Vedanta - The Priceless Jewel

I

Evincepub Publishing

Nehru Nagar, Bilaspur, Chhattisgarh 495001
First Published by Evincepub Publishing 2021
Copyright © Neera Manchanda 2021
All Rights Reserved.

ISBN: 978-93-5446-205-4

VEDANTA

THE PRICELESS JEWEL

NEERA MANCHANDA

IV

CONTENTS

VI

Let the sun filter in through the shimmering clouds to rest on your memorable and enchanting smile, forever encouraging the onlooker to continue his endeavours in the material and spiritual world to reach unspoken heights.

Dr. Vinay Srivastava you were to write the foreword for this very book as indeed you wrote for my last three books over a span of 5 years. Your insightful remark "Perfect" after going through Vedanta- The Priceless Jewel, I take as your most comprehensive comment of the level of understanding conveyed by the contents to you, the discerning reader.

Your loss is felt uncontrollably! May you bestow your blessings from wherever you are, on this book, the author and the reader and guide them to the fulfilment of the goal of Vedanta of self- Realisation in this life itself!

VIII

The wise owl presents this book as an offering to the seekers "who want to know"!

When night falls the world sleeps,

The owl alone does watch keep.

The phenomenal objects their attractions lose,

In deep slumber bliss all choose.

In nightly silence, silence speaks,

The owl he listens knowledge reaps.

Before the dawn has a chance to rise,

He listens, thinks and does imbibe.

The phenomenal world has come from Maya,

It will disappear in the elusive fire.

I am spirit pervading all,

Look out for me ere night doth fall.

Take up this book with an open mind. It is my attempt to bring before you the magic of the Bharatvarsh spiritual essence. Beginning with a brief look at some essential Vedantic concepts of I am Infinite, the Divinity I Am, Why Vedanta and how we can and should move on from Exclusivity to Inclusiveness in the first section; we reach a cursory understanding of the Vedas in the second section. This section further explains What Vedanta Is. By the time that one has perused the chapters on The World is an Appearance and

Prakriti and the Three Gunas, the intrinsic message of Vedanta is conveyed to the reader to work towards the goal of life- Self realisation to be achieved in this life itself!

Small write-ups on Mantras, fear and Maya bring further clarity to the reader's mind. Gurus from the authentic Vedantic tradition, who were steeped in the Upanishads and were themselves Realised persons left behind a legacy of talks, books, discourses, lectures and direction to enable the seeker come face to face with his Atman. Some of the stalwarts in this sphere were knocking at the mind's door for inclusion in this text and hence articles on Swami Vivekananda, Ramana Maharishi, Swami Chinmayananda and Swami Tejomayananda who is presently carrying on the tradition of Swami Chinmayananda are included in section three and may prove interesting reading.

The word Vedanta is explained in the spiritual texts as 'end of the Vedas', the Upanishads the philosophical portion of the Vedas. We know that Upanishads do not just provide what is termed as philosophy in the modern ages, but contain the experiences of the seers gained after tremendous, long and sustained Sadhana through self effort (Purushartha). Their realisation of the Atman lying within each one of us, being the same as Brahman, One without a Second, the Almighty, was shared by them with their disciples by word of mouth; till such time these experiences were put down on paper and became the Upanishads of the Vedas, now available to us. I am pleased to offer my understanding of the Kathopanishad, Mandukya Upanishad, Kenopanishad and Bhagwad Gita Upanishad in the fourth section of this book.

Most of the articles are interspersed with poems written by the author and relevant to the topics taken up and it is hoped that they will delight the reader and be an aid in getting closer to the essence of the subject undertaken. May your life be moulded on the path of Atman realisation.

THE AUTHOR INTRODUCES HERSELF

Born into a modern-day family where the food we ate was a blend of continental and Indian, vegetarian ad non-vegetarian. The clothes worn were both ethnic and western. The languages spoken amongst family members and friends were English by far with a little Hindi thrown in, as we needed to communicate with the retinue of servants. With a convent education as background, where the nuns discouraged us from speaking in Hindi, we even thought in English and translated the same mentally into Hindi, when we had to write an article on a given topic in school.

Father worked in an office with a ten to six routine. He adored his wife, incidentally our mother and they spent most of their time together visiting relatives and friends or inviting them over for meals. Official parties too were often attended by them. We four children were left more or less to our own devices once we returned from school, in order to keep ourselves occupied or in order to entertain ourselves. I, being the youngest spent most of my time outside the house with my friends playing a variety of games from 'stapoo' to badminton. Regarding our studies and manners we were brought up with the utmost discipline and strictness. This was an asset to us in later life.

Our parents were not spiritually inclined but lived according to the highest values. They were truthful to the core and held integrity, dedication and honesty in the highest esteem. Speech was controlled and no word or action was permitted that might hurt anyone. Behaviour towards those less fortunate than us in material comforts was always impeccable. These values were inculcated in the children as well. They believed that as long as one lived according to these values one did not need to be a temple goer or ritualistic, religious person.

The Almighty has his mysterious ways as he provided us with spiritual influence through the only grandparent we were to know. Our Nani (mother's mother) was a worldly-wise, yet very spiritual person. She worshipped Krishna and Guru Nanak and respected Ramakrishna Parmahansa and Swami Vivekananda and followed their teachings. A strong believer in Aum and the Gayatri mantra, she did 'havan' every single day of her life after taking her morning bath. She prayed and kept 'maun', silence for half an hour, every evening. Her smiling countenance shone with her inherent spirituality and attracted relatives and friends who sought her out for advice on worldly and spiritual matters.

We lost our father when I was eighteen years old, while our grandmother had passed away a year before. The spiritual and material protection that we felt so far, seemed suddenly to have evaporated. Life changed in imperceptible ways. It was then that one looked for an anchor, a support in life. A few years later marriage, children and a job brought with them their upheavals and responsibilities. Urgency was felt even more strongly to seek strength and guidance in day- to- day decisions and in defining long term peace. The outward fabric of existence was precarious. Finances and the attitude of people was diminishing and changeable. A sensitive soul felt unhappiness slowly wrap its shroud around it, taking it into an abyss of depression. An observant colleague handed over a copy of the Bhagwat Gita in English with Sanskrit shlokas(verses) and commentaries in English. It was the first ray of light.

The search for happiness in one's daily life is something everyone is familiar with. Each individual has his/her source of joy and plans his life years, months, days ahead based on what provides him happiness, joy or maybe contentment. Seekers of contentment are relatively few! Some find joy in travel, some in work of their choice, it could be computer programming, finance or the creative arts; while others, politics and status providing power. Still others were busy in pursuing knowledge or spreading the same. In the early days, knowledge was considered sacred and those who imparted the same, such as Brahmins and Gurus were revered. In our childhood teachers too were respected and even the written word was considered sacred.

Today the world has changed dramatically. Knowledge of the sciences, arts and what- have- you are available to all at the click of a button. The respect accorded to teachers, professors and lecturers is on the wane. Instant gratification is sought through the digital boom. Going a step further, AI or artificial intelligence has left the elder generation awed, while the younger generation no longer looks up to the elder generation or the scriptures to provide knowledge or guidance. The world is in a state of flux having lost its moorings and is floundering in the tempest of a new and as yet unstable intellectual environment. There is an explosion in communication channels like twitter and facebook bringing social media and the whole world into everyone's drawing room, leaving no option for deep thought before forwarding a response that may cause hurt, unhappiness or even lead to a mass movement in a negative direction. The stability of the past, rested largely on pursuit of knowledge in various fields, including perusal of scriptures, while living life based on values inculcated from family elders.

Knowledge then, now and in the future seems to be the basis for happiness, whether derived from Google, scriptures, elders in the family or gurus. Knowledge can be secular or spiritual. In the Sanskrit language it is known as gyan or vidya. The Vedas are ancient scriptures that are the first extant written knowledge available in India and probably in the world. Veda is derived from the root word 'Vid' which means 'to know'. India has a tradition of giving a new born child a name that is meaningful and often taken from the scriptures such as Vidyawati, my grandmother's name, which meant 'graced with knowledge' or the name of any of the Gods eg. Krishna, the God of preservation. The belief was that the name had a positive impact on the nature of the child/ individual. Thus, India the land of the Vedas had strong roots and despite suffering the onslaught of various invaders over centuries, could stand its ground due to the individual and collective strength provided by the teachings of the Vedas by way of mantras, hymns, rituals and traditions, theologies and philosophies extending to every aspect of life.

Before we move on to understanding the Vedas and what a vast and stupendous source of knowledge they provide, let us see where the term Vedanta came from. The last portion of each of the four Vedas is the philosophical portion called the Upanishads. 'Ved' stands for knowledge and 'anta' means the end. Thus 'Vedanta' means that spiritual knowledge provided by the end portion of the Vedas.

Section I
DIVINITY

THE DIVINITY I AM

I open my eyes and find myself in a space that is filled with alertness, acute awareness and tingling consciousness. Through this I come to calmness, peace and an accentuated sense of balance. Being at the centre of truth in its indefinable state, I am enveloped by bliss in all its divinity. A calm and pale light pervades the atmosphere and touches the core of my heart, filling it with serenity!

Here the author shares her feelings on Divinty through poetry:

Thoughts evade, while happiness pervades.

Desires dissipate, where desirelessness serenades.

Duality disappears, while oneness permeates.

I am one with the entire cosmos, the universe too rotates.

It is all a play before me, as I witness without haste.

There is no past or future, it is this moment I face.

Time is not a factor, to be considered any more.

I am all there is, time is now still.

Beyond causation, I exist for sure,

I was, I am and will be evermore.

Questions and answers about the why and wherefore,

Die a natural death, as the beginning, middle and end are within me and endure.

Do you recognise this state of everlastingness?

Soham...I am He. Satchitananda, Brahman, the ever free!

Vedanta tells you that this state is your destination and your goal, the state of everlasting happiness that you are looking for throughout life. At present, the happiness that you find is always short lived, followed by sorrow in equal measure. Vedanta offers you happiness that never ends, in fact, a state of continuous bliss. You are this bliss, but do not know it. Just remove the veil over your human eyes and seek within you. You will come face to face with who you really are - Divinity itself! No more birth and death. No more growing pains. No longer do you need to endure the feebleness of old age. The dualities of joy and sorrow, heat and cold, honour and dishonour, end. Equanimity reigns and serenity spreads. The dream is over and you come awake to realise your true Self!

WHY VEDANTA

The author is pleased to offer a short poem explaining why we should take up Vedanta and what it will do for us.

Vedanta the end of the Vedas,

To what end do I acknowledge Thee?

You express the Ultimate Reality Brahman,

Is it the Atman of which you speak?

All pervading, unchanging, omnipresent and omniscient,

Is that the light that ever shines within?

My mind and intellect roam where the sense objects are,

Were they all not meant for me?

The pleasurable often entices me,

Isn't the good dull and difficult to be?

So, Vedanta what do you say?

Why cannot I live indolently?

Spirit you are and spirit you will be,

Subtle mind, intellect both are matter definitely.

Strive for the Highest clutching Aum to thee,

Aum is Brahman and will set you free.

The most profound explanation about what Vedanta really does for us is that it presents the reality of an object before us. It does not create an object, nor does it create a particular aspect or quality of an object; instead it removes our false understanding about the object and reveals it to us as it is. An example of fire will enable us to understand its reality, as brought to our knowledge by Vedanta. Vedanta does not create fire but provides us with the knowledge that fire is hot and can burn; this is the intrinsic reality of fire. Whether we use it to cook or carelessly burn ourselves is up to us. In our ignorance we could imagine that fire is very pretty and could go too near it and burn ourselves. This is a simple and basic example.

The study of Vedanta requires a certain depth and seriousness of reading, listening, thinking and awareness so as to reach the essence of the subject at hand. Vedanta reveals the essence or reality of 'who I am'. The finite limited 'I' that is seen in the mirror, my body, is in reality the infinite 'I', the Atman. What a quantum jump Vedanta takes! It offers the explanation of how the knower (ME) becomes the known (pure knowledge). When we awake, we know the dream was not a reality and in comparison the awakened state is a reality. On a more serious note, when we realise our true nature as Brahman, the all pervading, unchangeable, omniscient and omnipresent, the little 'I', the individual becomes a part and parcel of my past ignorance. The knower has become the known, Brahman, that is, pure truth, intelligence and bliss.

We spend our lives running around trying to earn more and finding lasting happiness in family, friends, property, cars, etc. We all know that this happiness is an elusive thing. So, we are either looking for happiness or are pretending to be happy. Vedanta tells us that we are happiness itself. It goes even further and expresses that we are beyond happiness and are bliss, the condition of permanent joy. Vedanta reveals to us who we really are, as well as our relationship with the world and with the Almighty, the Supreme Reality, enabling us to relate and interact with them properly. It is not just dry knowledge or philosophy, but lucid and practical knowledge that dispels our ignorance and enables us to understand, verify and through logic, imbibe the Truth that we are Brahman itself. We are then in a position to reach Self Realisation, the final goal of existence, through Sadhana, the practical application and path as taught by Vedanta. Isn't it now clear as to 'Why Vedanta'!

I AM INFINITE

One of the truths accepted by Vedanta is 'I am infinite'. What do we understand by the terms 'I' and 'infinite'?

Let us take up the word **'infinite'** first.

Infinite is everlasting, not contained;

Not within the boundaries of time.

Infinite was, is and always will be

It is beyond space, extends everywhere,

Is not contained within an allotted space,

Nor is it restricted by any extraneous circumstances.

It is not finite, temporary or limited.

It does not have a beginning, middle or end.

The word infinite connotes expansiveness, limitlessness,

Impossible to measure or calculate,

It extends indefinitely, endlessly.

The next step is to understand what **'I'** means. We often hear the phrase "he has a lot of ego in him' or "he is full of attitude". Both phrases mean that he is proud. Should we therefore understand the word ego to be a negative term? **What exactly is ego, the 'I' we know?**

I, my name, address, designation,

Add to this any eminent relation.

Intellectual prowess, highly educated,

Creative, financially sound, elated.

I describe myself thus to the world around,

Ego and individuality appear without a sound.

Identifying with my body, I say,

This is who I am, each day.

Body is not complete without intellect and mind,

Ego is attached to all, three I find.

Notion of individuality is thus created,

Add attributes of the three, ego is thereby feted.

Ego in the relative world appears,

Same ego in the spiritual realm disappears.

Intangible yet powerful, with body identified,

Ego vanishes when mind and intellect ego decries.

Where does the ego begin? It begins with the word 'I'. In fact, ego is the 'I' that acts in the relative world. We identify with some form of our body, intellect or mind or any other feature of our character or nature, this identification gives rise to what is known as ego. This is what we understand as our individuality. Since ego is not something tangible, we cannot touch it. It is so subtle that when we try to reach it through our powers of analysis and intellectual understanding, it disappears. How does this occur? The moment we remove our identification with the attributes of the body, mind or intellect, we see that the ego has vanished. Once the ego vanishes, what is left is the real 'I', the Self or Atman.

Attached to the body we say "I eat" and "I am Arjun's mother". The first is an action the body performs and the second is a relationship one body has with another body, named Arjun. The instant we identify with the action of eating, I have conveyed that I am the doer and hence the results of enjoyment or discomfort are all mine and I must accept and bear it. The law of Karma prevails! As regards the identification of being Arjun's mother, one automatically becomes the recipient of all emotional upheavals or joy, as the case may be, due to the attachment. The identification with the body, mind and intellect ensures that I am living on the relative plane, with its accompanying sorrows and joys, pain and relief. This is called Samsara, the world of duality which keeps human beings on a see-saw of suffering, all due to the rise of the ego, our alter 'I'.

Vedanta clearly expresses that we are not the body, mind or intellect as these are made up of matter. Matter is changeable and temporary and irrespective whether it is in solid or subtle form, can give rise to pain; whereas the real 'I' is spirit, permanent, unchangeable and is pure bliss.

With this understanding of the words 'infinite' and 'I' how do we accept the Vedantic statement that 'I am Infinite', when I am caught up in the vicissitudes and struggles of life considering myself to be a puny individual in the hierarchy of existence, fighting against the powerful tyrants both at home and at work.

It is time now to move out of the present conditioned body and mind and see oneself not as the ego filled entity but as the infinite Aum; Aum the symbol of the Ultimate Reality-Brahman filled with light. When one visualises oneself as the symbol Aum, with one's eyes closed, one gets a sense of peace within and when one utters Aum and allows the sound of it to penetrate the mind, thoughts and very being, serenity pervades the individual. Concentrating the mind on the symbol at the point between the eyebrows, one continues to chant Aum, the very sacred symbol of Brahman. Inner peace and calm get hold of one as we slowly begin to feel expansive. One is no longer the puny self, one has become the symbol itself that expands and stretches beyond the confines of the physical body. The light of the symbol spreads in all directions and through this expansiveness, one experiences limitlessness. At this level of experience, one has gone beyond the confines of one's physical body and is experiencing infinity. This is an out of body experience that gives a glimpse of what one really is – 'infinite'.

We can know life in a relative plane of existence or spiritual existence only through what we experience within ourselves. In this case we know reality in the spiritual existence by what we experience through a meditation on Aum, undertaken within ourselves.

In order to get rid of the burden and bondage of the ego, what should one do? Quite simply, we have to remove the link of the 'I' with the body, mind, intellect and their attributes by accepting and understanding that 'I' the spirit or Atman is not the body, mind or intellect. The minute this clarity is felt, the ego will fall off, disappear or vanish. The notion of individuality will no longer abide. The question will then arise as to how can one function in the world without the ego, one's individuality. With the realisation that the ego related 'I' is not real and the 'I' as the Self or Atman is real and the only truth, one functions in the external world without attachment and with a serene, calm and balanced personality, understanding clearly that 'I am Infinite'!

A beautiful aid in probing, analysing and enquiring into the 'I- ego', is the element of love for the infinite 'I- Self'. By becoming the instrument of Brahman, we allow ourselves to be conduits through which Brahman works. Just like the flute that is hollow we can empty ourselves of all desires and thus permit the almighty Krishna to play his melodies taking us beyond the relative plane to his spiritual abode.

It is also beneficial to repeat to oneself often that 'I am infinite' so that we begin to mentally accept this Vedantic truth.

EXCLUSIVENESS TO INCLUSIVENESS

Today's modern society has changed vastly, from city collective consciousness to individual limited consciousness. It is transformed from a joint family, to a single unit of family. In some cases, the family has disappeared totally and live-in relationships have taken their place. The desire for a family is replaced by a stand- alone, or rather stay- alone individual. Slowly and steadily, the fabric of society or community consciousness has given way to an individual one. Needs are now personal, individual and unfortunately relate to oneself alone and are therefore selfish.

As long as success in finances and personal desires accrue, life goes on smoothly. The moment road blocks occur, mental stress with accompanying illnesses such as high blood pressure etc surface. Visits to the doctor are interspersed with bouts of unhappiness and possibly in case of extreme sadness, mental unbalance too. The need arises to stop and think. What is my goal? What are my ideals? Also, what are my values in life? Finally, why am I born as a human being and not as say, a goat?

We cannot live as an island distanced from the rest of the world. The individual is interlinked with other individuals in society, at the work place and even with the cleaner who cleans the house. Not only this, one is interlinked and interdependent with all facets of creation in one way or another. A simple example is, by breathing in oxygen and exhaling carbon dioxide human beings are connected to trees and nature. We need to eat, work and wear clothes; these are some of the basic requirements for survival. Now what about the most important aspect of our lives in the modern world, which is, mental health? The joy and happiness, peace and serenity necessary for the individual's spiritual and mental upliftment comes from an understanding that a human being is linked to and is one with all of creation.

The scriptures help us to understand who we really are, let us see how by an example. The waves of the ocean rise and surge and then subside back into it. The calm and peace of the depth of the ocean is not disturbed. The water that is the wave, melts down into the water of the ocean, whence it arose from. It is not possible now to distinguish the water of the wave, from the water of the ocean. Such is the case of each human being, rises at birth, spends its life span on earth and then goes back into its source, the Almighty. The individuality of that human being is no longer distinguishable. On the one hand all is water and on the other, all is spirit. The waves are the individuals and the ocean, the Almighty.

One has to live a pure, honest and unselfish life keeping the good of the whole society in mind and not just oneself. Such an attitude cannot exist without a heart full of love! This in itself would be the basis for happiness within a person. Instead of standing alone far removed from nature and human beings, if the following thoughts walked through one's mind, let us see the result. "I am not alone. I am one with all of existence. The sun, moon, stars, elements, birds, animals, plants and trees are all mine and I am theirs. What's more, all human beings and the almighty are within me and I am within them. I can no longer exclude anyone or anything for "I am All." The warmth and joy this brings to my very being is unsurpassable. I have moved from abject exclusiveness to total inclusiveness. The all of creation and the Creator himself are in me! We are all One. In view of this, an individual must accept where he is placed in life due to his past karma. He must handle the changed and changing circumstances in life that he has to face, from time to time, with strength and fortitude, keeping in mind that exclusivity will take him to sorrow and dejection, whereas inclusivity holds him in steady joy and contentment.

Is happiness our goal? What is happiness really? What does the word happiness connote?

I often hear management gurus say that we must seek out and achieve our goal within the next five or ten years. I have often wondered what this goal might be for me. What do we seek attaining, so that once achieved there is nothing left to reach out for? At this stage all aspirations and desires end. Life itself is fulfilled. Is it happiness?

A short story I read a long time ago helps us find the answer to this. A king with riches galore could not find happiness and someone told him that he should go to a wise man to seek his assistance in finding happiness. The wise man he met further sent him to Mullah Nasruddin. The king set out with a pouch full of gold and gems and rode his horse to the spot where Mullah was sitting, under a tree. The king dismounted from his horse and after greeting Mullah with a sad face, told him his predicament. In response Mullah jumped up, grabbed the pouch and ran into the by-lanes of the town. The king tied his horse to the tree and did his best to follow Mullah. He was unsuccessful, as he could not keep pace with the speed with which Mullah negotiated the lanes of the town he knew well. The king came back to where his horse was tied, sat down and cried his heart out. Not only did he not get an answer to his query but he had also lost his pouch of gold and gems. Soon Mullah came back to where the king was seated and handed over the pouch to him still full of the gold and gems.

The king was astonished but became very happy. Mullah then explained to him that happiness is part of the duality of happiness and unhappiness. To gain happiness one has to go through a lot of unhappiness. So, is it really worthwhile to seek happiness? Would it not be better to seek bliss? Bliss that has no opposite and is not a part of duality, has no highs and lows. It brings with it calm and serenity, peace and equanimity, continuity and everlastingness. Happiness on the other hand, is temporary joy, as unhappiness is waiting round the corner! Bliss transcends both happiness and unhappiness, as it rises above dualities.

Our contemporary spiritual giant, Sadhguru, has explained 'bliss' as "a sustainable level of pleasantness". Ecstacy, joy and happiness do not sustain and our emotions take us sometimes up and sometimes down, very much like a see-saw ride. Why should we not look for a permanent state of being, that provides steady and permanent bliss.

The path to this state of bliss is through Bhakti, Karma or Gyan marg. Sincere Sadhana leading to deep meditation helps one achieve the goal of Satchitananda; which is (sat) the Ultimate Truth, (chit) Pure Intelligence or Consciousness, (ananda) everlasting Bliss.

Section 2

THE WORLD AS SEEN THROUGH VEDANTA

VEDAS

In India the Vedas are regarded as revealed knowledge. For the Hindus they are their scriptures. At a time when man had not invented words and he ate, drank, slept and interacted with other human beings and animals with gestures; divine knowledge was revealed to him through exceptional personalities. These were seers with high receptivity, stupendous memory and superb understanding coupled with pure intellects and hearts. They assigned names to objects of their surroundings and these were incorporated in their explanations of the divine knowledge. Thus, the first concept of the human language came into existence in the revealed Vedas. The Vedic language is the mother of the Sanskrit language. Also, the Vedic verses are the earliest source of knowledge. The art of script and writing came about at a much later stage.

Before I go any further, let us see what the Vedas stand for. Having read only the English translations of a selection of verses from all four Vedas and also the commentaries of various spiritual giants on some of the Upanishads and Bhagwad Gita, I place before you a very rudimentary picture of what the Vedas indeed stand for and depict.

It is believed that nearly 99% of the written texts that comprised of the Vedas are no longer extant. These texts were cared for by families over years till either the texts or families or both were destroyed due to persecution by marauders of our land, then known as Bharat. Let it be clear that right in the beginning when divine knowledge was revealed to the Seers, the Vedas were not 'books' in the normal sense of the term. They were the accumulated treasury of spiritual laws discovered by different seers at different times. The sages and rishis of olden times went through severe tapas and Sadhana and realised these spiritual laws. They then passed them on to succeeding generations by word of mouth. It was much later that, when the written word was discovered, that these truths were put down on parchment paper. These rishis did not by far attach their names to them. It is only a disciple who may have assigned the name of his guru who had taught him a certain truth. The pure and egoless nature of those sages is evident from this. That was the time of Satya Yug, when honesty, purity, sincerity, dedication, love, compassion and strength of mind abound.

The Vedas are therefore considered revealed texts without beginning or end, dateless and timeless, containing truths provided to humanity by the spiritual realm, we may give it the name of God for our simplistic understanding. The word Veda is taken from the root Vid, which is knowledge or to know. Thus, the Vedas provide us with knowledge covering all aspects of our lives, that is, spiritual, mental, social, physical and behavioural.

The Vedas were classified broadly as Rig Veda, Sama Veda, Yajur Veda and Atharva Veda. Each Veda further consists of four sections, known as Samhitas (hymns), Brahmanas (rituals), Aranyakas (theologies) and Upanishads (philosophies).

Rigveda is the oldest available literature and as the word 'Rig' in Sanskrit means 'praise', the hymns, mantras or chants in it are expressions of worship and praise of the various deities or Gods of Vedic times, such as Surya, Indra, Agni and Soma by the devotees as friend, servant or child.

Samveda transforms the hymns of the Rigveda into musical compositions that emanate from the vibrations of the cosmos, bringing peace to the individual mind. The seven notes of music are derived from the Samveda. It is the main source of Hindustani music.

Yajur Veda is considered the source for performing all rituals or Yagna for prosperity. Even today a Hindu wedding or the cremation performed at death, is not considered complete if not accompanied by rituals prescribed by the Yajurveda.

Atharva, the word, means 'unchanging or unwavering' and Atharvaveda focuses on the universal truth of the oneness of the universe and how to live in touch with and finally merge with the Ultimate Reality. It also incorporates materialistic topics such as physiology, ailments and cures, society and its structure and the science of yoga.

It is believed that chanting the mantras of the Vedas, in the specified manner, brings about a change in the vibrations of the atmosphere there. Each Veda lays emphasis on a particular aspect of spirituality, that will enable a human being to move towards the central goal of self realisation. Rigveda indicates that praying for wisdom, inclination to perform good deeds, simplicity in temperament, keenness to serve humanity and through rejection of evil thoughts, we may attain immortality. Yajurveda invokes Lord Vishnu on the basis of mantras to grant both physical and mental resources, so that peace may prevail in the land, with people dedicatedly working for the good of all, both materially and spiritually. Samaveda prayers are to Agni for energy, Indra for strength and Soma to bestow calm and happiness. These were the Gods worshipped at that time. It was emphasised that learning to forgive, avoiding greed and anger and living according to truth alone would lead us Godward. Atharvaveda propounded remedies for evil and ill luck and specific mantras that when chanted, brought about healing and longevity. Also, prayers were mentioned for proper governance and protection from national calamities. Finally, and most importantly, an advice was given to worship and try and realise Omkar, as we are the children of the immortal.

The Vedas as a whole invoke one God, the Supreme Lord, who is the divine light behind all effulgences, through the Devas of Prakriti's bounties, such as the sun, wind and rain Gods. Vedas confirm that Devas are only an aspect of the one Supreme Lord. The Vedas do not praise human achievements, but ask us to establish a personal direct link with the Almighty, from our innermost being. It is suggested that we live as a valuable member of society, contributing to the common good. Values of life such as faith, austerity, generosity, peace, friendship, fearlessness and mutual understanding must be encouraged and lived by. God is, of course, the only pillar of strength we can rely on. Thus, the direct connection with God is emphasised, all else being of little or no value.

Now we come to an unique concept of the immortal soul (Atman), taking on the bondage of the human body and accepting the many such transitions to different bodies, as an acceptable benevolent bondage and thereby aiding the human being to reach final liberation! A quote from Pandit Satyakam Vidyalankar in his preface to The Holy Vedas sums up beautifully "The four Vedas contain the divine, infallible knowledge revealed ....to enlighten and spread Godly knowledge to man so that he may live a happy life in this world, be aware of his innate divinity and try to realise eternal bliss."

WHAT VEDANTA SAYS

In everyday life, we look outward and perceive through all our senses of sight, hearing, taste, smell and touch, the outside world. We accept that our perceptions are real and therefore the world is real. Next, due to our vasanas (desires) we interact with people, plants, animals, things in nature in order to obtain pleasure and happiness from them. Due to our sanskars (past karma) we sometimes get pleasure and happiness or sometimes pain and sadness. This is our samsara or the world we live in. Our belief that I am the doer or karta and I can control nature and the outside world to ultimately be powerful, rich and permanently happy is a delusion. As time goes on, life's circumstances take us on a roller coaster ride full of unexpected and uncontrollable events, filling us with agitations and anxieties for the present and future, coupled with memories of unhappy past events and emotions. At such times we stop and wonder: why me? Why am I only undergoing so much unhappiness when I have done nothing to deserve this?

At this point someone advises us that others too are going through tribulations in life, as it isn't smooth sailing for anyone. Thoughts such as, what is this world really about and why am I here in it and finally looking closely at myself, who or what am I, surge within me.

I stand in front of the mirror and see this personality that I love above all else. I may pretend that I love my spouse or children or particular friend or Guru more, but believe me, there is nothing in my consciousness that is more agreeable to my mind than I, myself. Thus, my body, my thoughts and intelligence that have so far been my guide, constitute who I am. In fact, the mightiest of the lot seems to be my mind, which is full of my special thoughts and intelligence that I pride myself on. I am also convinced that my mind has every right to exert emotions of anger or irritability whenever needed. Such an egoistic attitude can only lead to self destruction and unhappiness.

A proper understanding of this body, mind and intellect provided to us by nature will help us in moving towards right self expression and learning the real truth about ourselves and the world around us.

Let us first find out what exactly a mind is and where we can find it. A mind is a subtle entity compared to our body, which is solid. We can touch and see our body, our mind we cannot. If a few moments are spent in watching our thoughts, it does not take us long to realise that our mind is a continuous flow of thoughts that are far ranging and are normally not in an arranged sequence. In fact, the mind has been compared to a monkey that jumps from one topic to another with no connection between the content of either. Often enough, thoughts rush through without any interval and also connect with past memory of similar incidents or emotions. It is the mind that is the doer of all actions and is also the instrument of all our experiences. Without the mind, the body cannot act, as we know a man in coma is unable to do anything. When we are deep asleep, our mind is not available and it is as though dead. When we wake up from deep sleep, the mind slowly becomes aware of its surroundings and thoughts begin to rise up from the calm sea bed of the mind bringing activity and agitations back into our lives.

In dream sleep, the mind is active in imagination and creates a world which may be wonderful and full of pleasant occurrences or it may be upsetting and full of agitations. When we wake from dream- sleep, we slowly realise that what we went through was not real but only a dream and before we know it, thoughts of the previous day and impending activities planned for this day crowd our mind.

From the aforesaid it is clear that our mind is calm only when it is not activated by thoughts or imagination. Mainly in deep sleep.

The mind resides in our head and takes the help of its partner, the intellect, in taking decisions and thereby reacting or responding to the outer world. The intellect is even subtler than the mind and is positioned to delve into sanskars (past impressions) created by past experiences and stored in the memory portion of the brain. Based on it and the data provided by the mind and the senses, the intellect analyses the given situation. It then comes to a decision and directs the mind towards action.

The body, mind and intellect are all made up of matter. The difference between them is according to density and the functions prescribed to them by the cosmic order. While the body is made up of solid matter, the mind and intellect are made up of subtler matter. All material things of the world are made up of the panch tattva (five elements), earth, ether (generally understood as space), air, water and fire; our bodies too. Earth and water are heavier elements compared to the other three. Water comprises approx. 70 % of the human body and the food we eat forms the earth element. Air, space and fire (in the form of warmth) are within the human body in smaller percentages.

The mind is full of light thoughts that can travel through space. What we think permeates the space around us and affects the vibrations in the atmosphere. People with like-minded thoughts at a given time, imbibe those vibrations and thoughts. These in turn reinforce their thinking, be it negative or positive, loving or hateful. We see therefore how our every thought affects the universe around us. So not only should we stop and think before we act, but we should stop and think before we think! In fact, we should listen to the ever- subtle intellect and be guided by its suggestion made to the mind. It is now easy to understand why we need to calm our mind, as only a steady mind will implement the right decision.

Trying to understand matter through the body, mind and intellect which are nearest to us in terms of availability to study, we have a fair idea that matter is inert. But what makes this matter tick? How does it function? It is spirit that enters the inert human body and makes it come alive. This spirit is pure intelligence, it is pure truth and finally it is pure bliss. In one word it is Satchidananda. It is pure awareness and pure consciousness. For ease of study or understanding, it is called the Self.

Is the human body alone permeated by the spirit? No, the spirit is within all objects, things, animals, plants, etc in creation but their capacity to be aware of it is not there. They live and die totally unaware of the spirit within them. It is only the human being who can realise the Self within him. Not only this, Vedanta explains that he, the human being, is the Self itself! Vedanta also helps us ascertain that we are not the body, mind and intellect combine. The human being can attain self realisation in this life itself. What then is this spirit or Self that is also called Atman or Brahman? How do we reach it or find it, experience it and realise it? Vedanta is the path to knowing the real you, the Self. Once again, the question arises as to why

I should want to know my Self. The answer is overwhelming. Once such knowledge is achieved, ignorance disappears, equilibrium, balance, serenity, calmness, truth, peace and ultimate bliss are attained!

Vedanta explains what this ignorance is, that acts as a hurdle, to our being permanently in a state of bliss by experiencing the Self. We identify with our body, surroundings, position in life, material assets, family lineage and off- springs. This we believe is I or me. I and what I believe is mine make up my identity. This is ignorance. The real me is the Self within me. On gaining this supreme knowledge that I am the Self, the false identification with the body, mind and intellect disappears. That is, ignorance vanishes when knowledge appears. Just as darkness is dispelled when light appears. It is like waking from a long and deep dream and discovering that all that I held as real was indeed false and I am Pure Consciousness, Truth and Bliss and not this puny body. I was in bondage due to my vasanas (desires) which made me live in the world and enjoy or suffer the results of my past actions, as the merry go round of life took me.

The first prerequisite to stepping on the road to self realisation is the earnest desire to reach this goal. Do I really want to know who I am or am I satisfied with this merry go round of life leading to innumerable births and deaths, filled with sorrows and joys, pains and happiness at frequent intervals. Can I tear myself away from my attachment to my spouse, sons, daughters and grandchildren and many other relationships. Will my mind turn back often to my material possessions that I cannot part with and are the pride of my life? Yes, I must firmly put my mind at rest regarding all such attachments by being resolutely aware that these are all temporary, changeful and ultimately cause pain after providing short spurts of pleasure. If I am convinced that i want to find permanent happiness and peace, I need to walk on this path.

At first one is horrified at the prospect of giving up all possessions and loved ones. Slowly one realises that it is not necessary to walk away from all these and reside in the jungles or on mountains away from settlements. We need to steadily bring ourselves to understand the difference between the temporary and permanent, the changeful and the changeless, and the real and unreal. We can continue to interact with everyone and everything with the clear understanding that no one and nothing is permanently ours. We don't own them. The child born through us is given to us for a specific time for us to gain certain experiences in this life. We are required to nurture the child and bring him up to the best of our ability. He is not our possession or our slave and what we do for him does not entitle us to expect things in return from him. We came into this world alone and must live with aloneness. This will give us strength of purpose and help one to be clear headed and single pointed in one's search for one's Self. This does not mean that we must live with loneliness, as the cosmic order has placed us within a family unit and given us friends, colleagues and acquaintances to interact with during our lifetime but without attachment and expectations from them.

So, let us see how we can use Vedanta in daily life. Our perceptions gained through our five senses and sorted out by our mind and intellect, lead to awareness and knowledge. Our reactions and responses to these perceptions, ensure that we are active throughout life. We are aware that life's situations and circumstances keep changing and place challenges before us on how best to handle them, these can be at the work place or at home. In order to know the answer at any given time to a situation present before us, we need a clearly thought- out vision and philosophy based on inherent values that can guide us. Vedanta provides this to us. Understanding what Vedanta is, we are fortified with the necessary tools for facing life and its complexities.

One of the most important lessons one can learn from Vedanta is to depend on oneself for one's happiness. The happiness that we are seeking in the world around us, that is, from persons that we interact with and objects surrounding us, is only to be found within us. The joy of receiving love from relatives, friends, colleagues, members of our clubs or political parties is only temporary and selfishly motivated. Purchasing a car, house, television, the latest mobile or a piece of jewellery provides fleeting happiness. Permanent happiness or bliss is to be found from within oneself. Therefore, look within to find your real Self, is one of the first indications offered by Vedanta.

When we open our eyes to the outside world, we see a lot of variety and hence are led to believe that there are many diverse and colourful objects, animals, birds, insects and persons. Vedanta assures us that there is one thread immanent in all. Just as space is present everywhere and everything is present within it. thus the 'One' is present in the 'many'. This one is also called the Ultimate Reality, Brahman, Atman, Self or Pure Consciousness which permeates all existence and all existence resides within it. Since it is my Self, I am that too. I cannot dislike or hate anything or anyone, as it would amount to hating myself!

Knowing that everything and everyone around me and even far away from me, is me alone, loving one to the exclusion of all else, seems pointless, be it person, animal or object. If I must be attached, I must be attached to all of existence. If not attached, then, one would need to be to all of existence. Non attachment instantly removes pain, sadness, unhappiness and provides peace, equanimity, serenity. It also helps one to begin accepting life situations as they present themselves. Agitation and disturbance of mind, no longer assail us. With the wisdom gained through the principles imbibed from Vedanta, we are amply strengthened to tackle life.

PRAKRITI AND THE THREE GUNAS

What the three gunas or qualities are, is expressed in the following poem by the author.

Sattva, Rajas and Tamas in me.

Sattva I am today, light and clearheaded, I sail away,

Goodness, love and compassion travel with me,

Shraddha and faith permanent companions they be,

Peace, serenity, calmness are my shadows, you see,

Keeping all within me, content and free.

Enveloped in activity **Rajas** is me,

In -filled by desires, I cherish with glee.

I worship demigods to grant my wishes for free,

They adore my strength, sincerity and activity.

Restlessness is my watchword I say,

Leading to movement and actions each day.

Mindful of the goals to achieve,

Vigour and forwardness are my steps to succeed.

Brahma, the creator has been my guide,

Being the king of Rajas, he does not let me slide.

Enough of activity, energy and gain,

I am **Tamas** slothful, dull and plain.

Deceit and darkness lie in wait,

Wherever I live, slumber, deny or negate.

Accept me as I am, for I am lazy and hate change,

I kill and destroy ruthlessly and let the morrow rearrange.

The buds will flower, the birds will sing,

The sun will rise, a new morning bring.

The ancient Sankhya philosophy divided existence into Prakriti and Purush. Prakriti is to be understood as matter and Purush as spirit. Matter being inanimate, is activated by the presence of Purush (spirit). Another term that is in common usage in the English language for Prakriti is 'nature'. In fact, nature surrounds us in the form of trees, mountains, etc, as solid matter and the nature of a human being is within him as subtle matter, that is visible through his behaviour, speech and actions. Thus, the words Prakriti, matter and nature are often used interchangeably. There is an even subtler element, the spirit, Purush or soul, that makes their qualities or gunas of Sattva, Rajas and Tamas seemingly come alive.

The Vedantist rejects the idea of soul and nature being totally independent and separate, as it is difficult if not impossible to bridge the gap between them. Vedanta affirms that both are in fact one. Thus Purush, atman, soul, or spirit is one and appears as the many of Prakriti or nature. More of this later. Let us understand what Prakriti really is and how we should deal with it in life! For this we need to treat Prakriti as separate from spirit.

We know that Prakriti is matter, as we see it in our external world. Inspired to write a poem, the author shares it with the reader.

Prakriti, the name is as dainty as a flower.

It covers all of nature, rain and heavy shower.

A butterfly takes wings when the cuckoo sings.

The mountains glow in the rising sun's fire.

Waves leap and throng the rocks, they so wrong,

Spitting white foam, as they laugh along.

Stars abound in the firmament above,

Staring down at the green grass, tree and shrub.

Prakriti, thy name so sweet,

Takes my breath away, when you, my eyes do meet.

In you do I see my God Almighty,

Calm, serene, pure, blissful holding me lightly.

Through your many facets, colours and grace,

A glimpse of the everlasting spirit I trace.

Gentle breeze sets my heart aflutter,

Caresses the tree tops as the birds begin to twitter.

Prakriti with my eyes open wide,

I cannot but love thee, as the waves, the tide.

When we look around us, we find that each human being is different in temperament and attitude. His tendencies and approach to life, actions, emotions, responses and reactions vary from person to person. How does this come about, we may wonder! Their nature is made up of three qualities or gunas that is, Sattvik which is good and pure, Rajsic which pushes man into intense activity and Tamsic which makes him lazy, slothful and deceitful. Each person has all three gunas in him in some measure. Any one guna may predominate and the person may overall be seen, as say a Rajsic person, if he is found to be tremendously active. However, any guna may be in the ascendency at any given time of day or year. Even though one of the gunas is more or less prominent and classifies his overall personality, still even during twenty- four hours, the three gunas will be active, one suppressing the other two for a while. The main distribution of gunas in a person is based on his past sanskars, his past impressions stored in his memory based on actions and experience from past lives. In this way, each individual is unique.

A little self introspection can reveal where one's tendencies lie. This can enable one to make concerted efforts to improve one self and increase the quantum of Rajsic and then Sattvic qualities in one's nature. In order to move on the path of self realisation, we need to begin at the beginning viz. understand our own nature. The first goal is to reach the highest guna, Sattvic guna, as far as possible. This can be achieved by constant watchfulness of what we think and do. Choices must be made at every step of our lives, in order to take us towards honesty and truthfulness, and unselfishness, putting thou before oneself.

It is important to understand that the Self or Atman does not act in the world. It is a witness before which activities occur, in its presence. The gunas function in the presence of the spirit, Purush or Atman. The Atman does not act at all. It IS. Just as the sun high up in the sky full of light and heat, does not act but is only a witness, while beings and plants, earth, air and water, animals and humans thrive in its presence. The gunas of nature act similarly in the presence of the Atman. If the Atman leaves the body, the body is once again inanimate matter and the gunas or qualities of Prakriti also subside.

What then is acting in the world, we ask. In the presence of Atman or pure consciousness as the witness, it is the gunas in one that are interacting with the gunas in another. Thus, the gunas in nature are bringing about action and changes in life. The gunas are subtle and form the nature of each human being. When the gunas in one person interact with the gunas in another, we call it interpersonal relations. All action therefore occurs in Prakriti.

A closer look at the three gunas will prove beneficial in understanding Prakriti better. Sattva brings out goodness, compassion, charity and love in a person and is therefore considered as purity and luminosity. It however has an attraction towards knowledge and due to this, it still binds us! Rajas goads us to action for personal gain and for fulfilling desires. Due to its attachment to action and the ego, Rajas makes a person feel that he is the doer (karta). The Karta is also the Bhogta (sufferer or enjoyer) and thus Rajsic action normally results in pain. Tamas makes the person indulge in laziness and lethargy and can even lead to actions with evil intent and is therefore darkness, leading to negligence and ignorance.

Understanding the nature of each guna minutely, helps us to watch and monitor ourselves and bring about transformations in our day- to- day life; rising slowly from the Tamsic level to Rajsic and then to Sattvic temperament. When we reach the stage where inertia is absent, selfish desires are extinct and the good of all is uppermost in our minds and hearts, this is the moment for Prakriti and its qualities to disappear and the Atman in all its glory to appear.

These three gunas tie the body, mind and intellect to bondage. To rise above bondage, we need to transcend the gunas and become Trigunatita. In other words, Tamas must change into tranquillity and peace, Rajas into tapas and austerity and Sattva be sublimated into the pure light of consciousness. Man is then Triganatita, as he has gone past the three gunas.

Going beyond the three gunas, the common man turns into a Yogi, as he takes the final leap from Sattvic temperament into pure consciousness, transcending the very mind and intellect that brought him to this level. Honour and dishonour, friend and foe are the same to him. He no longer feels that he is the doer and accepts that the gunas interact with the gunas only.

The human being thus leaves behind the cycle of birth and death, feebleness of old age, the agony of illnesses and the pain and unhappiness that tormented him during the ups and downs of life. He is one with Satchidananda, the ultimate truth, pure intelligence and bliss.

The three gunas are present in every aspect of our lives. We can consider them as the three tendencies of nature and can visualise them as the "three strands making up the twisted rope of nature". S. Radhakrishnan goes on to say that even the cosmic trinity reflects the predominance of one of the gunas, as Sattva in Vishnu who is the preserver, Rajas in Brahma who is the creator and Tamas in Shiva the destroyer.

In fact, we are what our faith or shraddha is. Let us clear the meaning of faith as it is meant here. It is not blind acceptance of a belief. "Faith is striving after self realisation by concentrating the powers of the mind on a given ideal." How we do this depends on our nature viz. Sattvic we worship God in form or without form, Rajsic we worship the demigods for fulfilment of our desires and Tamsic are those persons who undertake self torture and form a cult of departed spirits. Vedanta does not encourage or admire self torture or severe asceticism. Similarly, food, sacrifice, penance and gifts are also categorised under the three gunas of Prakriti and our daily lives are affected by how we undertake them.

Being aware of the intricacies of these gunas in every action in our lives, leads us to attempt to move up the ladder from Tamas to Rajas to Sattva in all aspects of life. Without realising it, we are climbing the ethical ladder. On getting a firm hold on Sattva, the need to transcend it and move on to the spiritual pinnacle is helped by the mystical saying 'Aum Tat Sat', the threefold symbol of Brahman. Aum is God Almighty or pure consciousness or eternal light. Tat is that stage beyond even cosmic consciousness and is also the Turiya or fourth stage, which comes after the three states of cosmic living viz. waking, dream and deep sleep. Sat is the Pure reality or the only truth. All that is good in penance, faith and gifts, or any action in this regard is called Sat. Anything that is not good in any aspect of our lives, is called Asat. The phrase 'Aum Tat Sat' is used to sanctify all Sattvic actions and thus our thoughts rise above the mundane when we utter this phrase, as the depth of meaning makes us soar above and beyond our day- to- day existence.

Our spiritual journey cannot begin without an in depth understanding of the three gunas and how they permeate our lives. Only then can we transcend Prakriti to reach Purush, Spirit, Atman and the Universal Brahman!

MANTRAS

Since a lot has been said regarding mantras in the Vedas, it would be useful to understand what the word 'mantra' stands for. Mantras are revealed truths. They were revealed to ancient sages (Rishis) after they had undertaken intense meditations and austerities. They are not theories or philosophies developed by a human mind or intellect but are divine revelations. Mantras are therefore classified under Shrutis, which means, 'that which was heard'. They are words with deep meanings. They are very importantly, vibrations also.

In fact, when a mantra is chanted properly, the vibrations it produces in the mind, match with the essence of the mantra and we experience that essence. To explain further, if the mantra is chanted intoning the correct sound, with total concentration, the deity or law of the mantra reveals itself to the chanter of the mantra. A mantra must be chanted with sincerity and devotion. Through mantra chanting, a specific sound vibration of that particular mantra, helps the mind to vibrate at a certain frequency and the mind then experiences the essence of that mantra. The Deity blesses the chanter with the boon mentioned in that mantra, for example, long life or moksh (liberation). The mantra also protects the person who recites and reflects on it. A mantra is thus a very powerful medium to reach out to the Ultimate Reality, be it for a boon for this life or for spiritual guidance for self realisation.

Mantras are often used for purposes of Jaap; repeated rendition of the mantra strengthens the mind and purpose of the sadhak and helps him in concentration and single- pointed access to the essence of the mantra.

MAYA

Maya is the creative energy that formulates a variety of forms in our mind or consciousness. The universe is one such example which is made up of millions of forms. Where does Maya come from? It is the shakti or strength of the Self or Brahman. It is within pure consciousness. Since Brahman is the Ultimate Truth, Maya too is reality when seen from the point of view of Brahman. However, what it creates, that is, forms, are an illusion as the ultimate reality is Brahman alone.

Brahman or Self is one and is only projected as many. The many are projected through Maya. When we look out through our senses, especially the eyes, we see objects of a variety of forms which are changeable and impermanent. We therefore find it difficult to accept them as real, as the Self when looked at from the spiritual point of view, is permanent, eternal and unchangeable. Thus, when viewed in this manner the objects seem like an illusion created through the power of Maya. Is Maya then ignorance and a negative power? No, it isn't. Maya is a reality. It is the active strength of the Self. It projects the vision envisaged by the Self. We, as humans, think and plan certain projects and our energy implements them as actions, to create say a building or a painting or any work of art. Similarly, when the Self has to act, it uses the Maya strength or Maya energy to implement the same. Hence Maya is a positive energy and a reality. Haven't we in India heard the phrase-'Ishwar ki Maya' translated in English it means the 'power of God'. It is important to keep in mind at all times that the Self is one and is pure consciousness or awareness.

When we think of the world as an illusion and not real, we must understand that the world has a relative existence. The substratum for it is the Self. Maya is an illusion, as the Self is the Reality. The world can also be interpreted to be a reality, since it is projected by the Self (Brahman) through its Maya shakti. In much the same way, the human being is real, as created by the Self or Brahman with the Atman or Self at its core. It can also be viewed as an illusion, as the body, mind and intellect are all changeable and impermanent and so unreal.

It is when we look within through sadhana, concentration and meditation that we realise for ourselves that the substratum for the world is Brahman and the core for the human being is the Atman. Brahman and Atman being one and the same and the only reality, Maya the shakti (power) ultimately dissolves into the pure consciousness that is Brahman and is no longer visible.

FEAR

At any given time in life and at any particular position or status, we find that we are fearful; fearful of physical injury to our person or to our family members. We fear that our possessions may be taken away by theft or they may be damaged. We therefore take precautions, such as putting iron grills around the house or flat where we stay. Place precious jewellery and important papers in lockers or locked cupboards. Domestic staff is admonished to be careful in speech and action. Fire and general insurance for residence, life insurance for self and family members, add to the steps taken to safeguard life and property. We also fear that we ourselves and those that are precious to us may get mentally assaulted at work place, in school or college.

Where does this fear emanate from? Upanishads state that duality is the cause of fear. In this relative world where we believe that we exist together with innumerable persons, animals, birds, reptiles and the five elements, besides other planets and possibly unknown beings on them too! In such a scenario fear of all the known and unknown, we consider as natural or normal. The other may cause hurt or injury to me due to dislike, jealousy, hate, greed or passion. When we see the world as different from us, we are frightened as we feel lonely and alienated, as the thought of the other causes fear.

How can we dispel this fear and live with equanimity and peace? Vedanta emphasises that realisation of the truth that 'I am the Infinite Truth and the world is not different from me' is the solution for this problem. I, myself, am appearing as the world and the various beings and things in it. Thus, whom or what should I fear? Vedanta does not tell us that this world does not exist but that it is an appearance that is projected by, exists in and finally merges back into, the real 'I' or Brahman. On the absolute level, Brahman, I and the world are one infinite existence, the one Truth appearing as all three!

In the physical and mental world what is known is different from the knower, for example, knowledge that a bird is flying makes one aware of the bird but does not make one the bird! However, on the spiritual level, on gaining pure knowledge of the Self, one instantly realises that one is the Self itself! One does not gain partial knowledge of the Self but the knower wholly becomes the known or rather he realises that he was always the Self/ Truth/ Brahman. Once gained, this knowledge is never lost or forgotten. Fear can never enter the mind of such a Realised person. He lives in peace and calmness for the rest of his life on earth.

THE WORLD IS AN APPEARANCE

Starting from the premise that I am Brahman, the only Truth, it follows that all else is false or at best only an appearance. Accepting the most important precept of Vedanta that the real 'I' is Brahman, it is around us, near us and within us; and ultimately, we accept that we and Brahman are one and the same. The 'we or I' mentioned here, does not mean our personality or the individual identity made up of body, mind, intellect attached with the ego. In fact, it indicates the real Self or Atman. When I and Brahman, the pure super-consciousness are one and the same and there is only one Reality, it therefore follows that all else does not exist.

On the relative plane we find this truth difficult to accept. With all our sense faculties of sight, hearing, taste and touch we experience the world and its variety from moment to moment. There is little doubt in our minds that the things of the world seem solid, liquid or gaseous to our sight and touch, pretty or hideous to our sight depending on the picture present before us at any given time and musical or horrendous, as the sound touches our ear drums now and then! Thus, we interact with the external world of things, animals and human beings between birth and death. Here we once again understand 'we' and 'I' to mean the body, mind, intellect and ego combine. This then is the world we are familiar with. For us this tangible world is our real world.

We are aware of this world when we are awake. Now let us look at our dream world. Taking a pleasant dream as an example, where one has purchased a new flat with all the latest designer fittings, a modular kitchen, the view of a golf course from the window and a swimming pool below, one is delighted. While swimming with a daughter, on a hot summer day, enjoying the cool water of the pool, the insistent ringing of the doorbell wakes one up to the reality of the old house in the middle- class colony! We need to analyse whether the dream was a reality or the present time is real. Since we live through a different dream each time but wake up to the same surroundings and existence, we readily accept the waking state as a reality and the dream state as a temporary appearance.

Walking back at night from work one day, if one sees a strange tall man standing ahead on the sidewalk, one would be a bit terrified if one is not accustomed to being out at night. The first reaction would be to cross over to the pavement on the other side. Now if the street lights were to come on suddenly and reveal that the strange man was indeed a lamp post, one would be relieved and feel a bit foolish at the same time! When we do not have complete information or knowledge about a situation, we imagine something other than the reality. In this case the strange tall man was superimposed on the lamp post. The lamp post was a reality and the man was just a false appearance.

These examples of the relative world help us to understand the deep truths of the spiritual world. Brahman, Atman, Self, soul, spirit, pure consciousness, pure intelligence, pure bliss, God or Ishwar are some of the different names for 'That One Reality'. This Reality is the substratum of the world as we see it and experience it, with our sense faculties. This world includes all of earth, all the planets, elements, beings and things sentient and insentient. It is for us to realise the truth of what and who we really are. Once we reach Self- Realisation and know that 'I AM' permanent and all else is only temporary and part of the cycles of projection, preservation and dissolution, the world as we see it will be clearly accepted as an appearance within time, space and causation.

Brahman is Satchitananda. Sat means truth, chit is consciousness and ananda is bliss. Thus, Satchitananda means pure truth, pure consciousness and pure bliss. Brahman and Atman are one and the same. Since the real 'I' is Atman, it is therefore correct to conclude that in essence I and all human beings are in reality Brahman. Brahman is infinite, which means limitless and unbounded. Anything with form has a boundary and is therefore bounded or limited and thus human beings in their physical presence or form are limited. It is their real Self or Atman that is unlimited or infinite. Since there cannot be two infinites, it is accepted that there is only one Brahman and therefore all human beings are really one with Brahman.

Brahman is the efficient cause of all sentient beings and things, as well as all material things. Thus, the world that we know, that exists within the parameters of time and space, with names and forms, colours, smells and variety is brought into existence by Brahman. The question that arises is does Brahman change into all human beings, animals, plants, trees, mountains, rivers and elements? If that were true, it would be impossible to accept Brahman as the only Reality or Truth. Though Brahman is indescribable, yet certain words are in use to bring the human mind closest to understanding Truth, such as omniscient, omnipresent, unchangeable and infinite. So how can one explain Brahman being the cause of this world that we perceive and experience, which is made up of sentient and insentient beings and things? Since Brahman is unchangeable it cannot change to become this world. It is the unchangeable substratum of the changeable world! The world is a superimposed appearance on Brahman, just as the snake is a superimposed appearance on the rope in the example where the rope is imagined as a snake in the darkness. Another example of the changing scenes of a film on the blank white screen which serves as the substratum, help one to understand that the world is temporary and only an appearance.

Vedanta provides the firm conclusion that all beings appear from Brahman and exist and dissolve in it alone. The Upanishads are the philosophical portion of the Vedas and are also known as Vedanta. They are the Anta of Veda or end portion of Vedas. They confirm again and again that the world and the cosmos are projected by Brahman, exist in it and finally merge back into it. The ocean too projects innumerable waves which exist for a time and then merge back into the ocean. This is an on-going process. The waves and water remain as water, which is their essence throughout. Similarly, every being, object and even thought emerges and then merges back into Brahman continuously.

Dreams too are projected by the waking mind and after the dream has existed for some time, it merges back into it. The waking mind alone is the creator, maintainer and destroyer of the entire dream. It alone is the material and sentient cause of the dream. It is the waking mind that appears as the dream world and the dream world is only an appearance. The essence of all the beings in the dream world is the waking mind alone. The snake is not different from the rope. The dream is not different from the waking mind. The world is not different from the Truth or Brahman. The superimposition does not have a separate existence from the substratum. They are essentially one.

While the world that we experience as the individualistic ego, body, mind and intellect combine, is only an appearance on the realistic level; the real Truth, Consciousness and Bliss combine- Brahman is the permanent essence of all. Brahman exists in the heart of all beings as their own Self. 'I am the Infinite Truth' is the very essence of Vedanta.

Section III

THE GREAT MASTERS

SWAMI VIVEKANANDA'S VIEWS ON THE UNITY BEHIND DIVERSITY

Placed below is a poem written by the author as an offering to the revered Swami Vivekananda and his guru, Ramakrishna Paramhansa.

Naren finally you have come to me,

Said Ramakrishna to our Swamiji.

Looking for God? he questioned him severely,

Have you seen God personally?

Yes, said Ramakrishna, as I see you before me.

His search ended. Vivekananda acknowledged his guru.

Strength is life, weakness is death,

Was his motto till his last breath.

He crossed the oceans to the west,

The first spiritual guide, it was his test.

He spoke as an orator at the Parliament of Religions in 1893,

To loud applause that resonated unendingly.

A champion of Vedanta, he gave us the pure formless One,

The Ultimate spirit, once realised, then all is done.

We are the children of immortal bliss,

Not sinners, but divine pure Atman within.

So let us heed his clarion call to each one, he truly briefed:

Arise, Awake and stop not till the goal is reached.

Swami Vivekananda was one of the greatest proponents of Vedanta of his times and what he said is relevant even today. He explained what Vedanta stood for in the simplest of terms, removing the complexities that so confounded the student of Vedanta.

When going through Swami Vivekananda's lectures as published in the complete works of Swami Vivekananda by the Ramakrishna Mission, we find that the words are so profound and powerful that to think of substituting them with one's own seems blasphemy. Thus, much of this chapter carries quotations by Swamiji in order to keep the character and depth of his thoughts intact. "Unity is knowledge, diversity is ignorance." Swamiji takes us from ignorance to knowledge and darkness to light.

Brahman is the substratum, the blank white screen, on which the universe in its variety is superimposed temporarily as a film. Brahman appears as the universe but is in reality omnipresent and omniscient, eternal, unchangeable and infinite. Brahman is the denominator and the various facets of the external world are numerators; such as planets, sun, moon, earth, human beings, animals and elements. Brahman is the unity behind the external world as we see it. Brahman is also the Self or Atman within human beings and all living things.

There is only a difference in the level of manifestation, from the lowest to the highest.

Swami Vivekananda explains that Vedanta is all inclusive and accepts the evolution from Duality to Advaita, as lower truths to higher truths, but truths none the less, in the spiritual development of human beings through the ages. They are, in fact, stepping stones, as the human being went further up the spiritual ladder in his enquiry into the reality of his inner being. Vedanta presents Brahman, the impersonal unity, behind diversity. He also states that Vedanta does not require a book or personal God, as the spiritual precepts given in the Vedas are eternal laws that have always existed and are not restricted to any one human being or person.

Vedas are the revealed spiritual and religious documents of the people of India. They are available to all persons who accept them as such and are willing to treat them as the final authority in spiritual matters. Vedas are broadly divided into the Karma Kanda (action and ritual portions) and the Gyana Kanda (knowledge and spiritual portions). Karma Kanda is in use presently for marriage, death and other such rituals. Our concern here is with the Gyana Kanda which comprises of the Upanishads, also known as Aranyakas and Vedanta. They are placed at the end of the Vedas, hence the name Vedanta, veda + anta (end).

Rishis of yore were spiritual discoverers. They undertook deep and prolonged Sadhana before they achieved enlightenment. This they shared with their students and over time these were written down as Rishi and student dialogues that we know today as the Upanishads. These gems of wisdom were translated and commentaries were written upon them by Shankaracharya, Ramanujam and others and thus are available to us today. As per Swami Vivekananda, the term Vedanta covers and includes the Upanishads, the Sutras of Vyasa and the Bhagwad Gita.

Swamiji clearly states that Divinity is within each one of us. "Every being is the temple of the most high." The goal is to manifest this Divinity. He goes on to say that we are all one. We are not individual souls but the same One exists in each one of us. The Sanskrit word for this One is Brahman. We normally refer to Brahman as 'God', as we are familiar with this term in normal usage. Brahman is all there is. It appears as the various phenomena in this universe. The sages of old times declared "Ekam Sadu Vipra Bahudha Vadenti" meaning "He who exists is one, sages call him variously".

The human being is thus raised to the level of pure divinity. He is not a sinner and does not commit a sin. He may have been ignorant and therefore may have made mistakes in his life. The real nature of a human being is the Perfect Infinite One, ever free, beyond all compare, unchanging, bliss absolute and pure consciousness – Brahman. Goodness and purity are our nature and cannot be destroyed. The goal presented by Vedanta is freedom. In order to reach this goal, the first step is to believe in oneself. This faith in one's innate purity will provide the strength to live a life of feeling, compassion and love in this phenomenal world, as hurting or hating anyone would amount to hurting oneself, as we are all one and the same.

Since ignorance leads to mistakes and sorrow, Vedanta insists on oneness, for then love expands to include all. We are the unlimited in reality but when we limit ourselves to this body, the cause of all evil or rather ignorance residing within us such as, envy, selfishness, hatred and the greed for acquisition rise up and our actions are swayed by them. Forgetting our real nature, we think and act and are resultantly miserable in the long run, to our utter astonishment! The theory and effects of karma are conveniently forgotten! As per Swamiji such errors are low degrees of manifestation and we must manifest in higher degrees. It is a fact that we are Infinite and therefore self-realisation as Brahman is possible for each and every one of us. When we feel for others, we are growing in oneness. Feeling is life, strength, vitality and since we are Brahman which is the only Truth, we must feel it intensely. Swamiji says "You are That already. Only know it."

It is most significant to remember that "affirmation of our divinity does not apply to the phenomenal but to the noumenal." In order to strengthen our thought process towards the noumenal world, we should repeat "Aham brahm Asmi" which means "I am Brahman" or "Soham", "I am He" to ourselves. This position is not valid in the phenomenal or external world as we cannot proclaim that I am God and go about doing as we please in the world of senses. Vedanta states that sense enjoyment is not the goal, as real happiness is beyond the senses. Morality too is not the goal of man but the means through which freedom is attained. Nirvana is the realisation of the Self. It can be attained here and now and one does not have to wait for death, to reach it. The one on the path of Gyan is impatient and cannot wait. Thus, the Gyani wants to achieve immortality now itself.

One needs to understand that one is not just this little body but is the essence of the whole universe and one can spread one's arms out, to clasp the whole universe to one's self, through sheer bliss. We are pure spirit and only spirit, the only Truth and Infinite. The universe is the spirit (Brahman) appearing as the various elements, beings and things of the universe. The universe and all its material bodies exist temporarily and then become finer and finer till they subside for a time, become motionless and are then projected once again according to their cycle, Pralaya. Thus, they are changeable and impermanent.

Only the spirit is permanent, does not expand or contract, nor does it come and go, it is never born nor dies. It is indestructible and omnipresent. The Vedantist believes that birth and death are changes in nature and reincarnation is the evolution of nature.

Swami Vivekananda was critical of the modern ideas of excessive caring of the human body. He proposed that one give up selfishness, as Vedanta is concerned only with spirituality. He said "what makes you different from me? Body and nothing else. Forget the body and all is spirit!" With the awareness of the body and identification with it, come all concerns for me and mine. Vedanta formulates universal Oneness , not universal brotherhood as do other religions. The ideas of family brother, caste brother and national brother are barriers to realisation of Vedanta. We are, therefore, required to feel sympathy through the whole universe and not only through one body and its relationships. Vedanta provides a higher ideal and asks us not to give up the body but to "transcend it". We need to go beyond this little body and embrace the body of the whole universe as 'me'. A very profound and gigantic thought, but achievable. Selflessness is the perception of the universal, not of the individual – Not I but Thou.

Swami Vivekananda revered the old Indian religions as better than the "modern system namely competition and gold". He felt that nothing can be done without renunciation. In order to help others "the little self must go". "Feel for others till you realise you are all parts of one whole, Brahman." Therefore "awake, arise and stop not till the goal is reached". He also emphasised that knowledge of the meaning of Om, "It is Brahman, greatest reality" and awareness that "I am Om" will lead us to guide others on the spiritual path that they too are Brahman, by telling them "Tat Tvam Asi" meaning "That Thou Art". He believed that the person who has acquired the sameness, accepting the same divinity is in the lowest animal and highest priest, has even in this life conquered all existence.

The greatest deterrent in following the path declared by Vedanta is our love for our identity, our individuality, this Nama Rupa or name and form, our body, mind and intellect. There is a Hindu legend where one of the gods incarnated as a pig and joyfully lived the 'piggy' life with his pig family. Seeing that he had lost awareness of his real nature, the other gods cut open his pig body and out emerged the god quite astonished that he had merrily lived a pig's life. Such are we! Quite forgetful of our reality as the Self or Atman, we adore our 'pig' bodies on earth.

If we take away the form and name from a thing or body, what we are left with is spirit alone. Form and name are given to sentient and insentient beings in the external world by Maya, the power or energy of Prakriti or Nature in order to bring about differentiation and variety. The essence or substratum of the universe is spirit or Brahman alone. We are all incarnations of Brahman. The human body is the only temple with the spirit (Brahman) within it. All our prayers are answered by Brahman within us.

The Vedantist believes that the individuality we have, is a delusion. As everybody is continuously changing, our body, mind and intellect which are also changing, cannot be our permanent and real identity. Also, the human body finite in nature is perishable. Beyond it is our spirit, Self, Atman, Brahman by whichever name we refer to it, that is unchangeable and Infinite. The body cannot be infinite too as two infinites cannot exist. Thus, there is only one real and infinite 'individual' i.e. Brahman. Brahman is all that exists.

A very pertinent fact has come to light that the God of Vedanta is principle, not person. In Swami Vivekananda's own words, "He is the infinite impersonal being, ever existent, unchanging, immortal, fearless and you are all His incarnations, His embodiments." He is the reality, ever blessed, ever pure and perfect. "This is the God of Vedanta and His heaven is everywhere. Worship everything as God - every form is His temple." "Proclaim the God within you, do not deny him."

The Vedantic idea is to raise all humanity slowly and gently towards the realisation of that great ideal of the spiritual man, who is non resisting, calm, steady, worshipful, pure and meditative. The Upanishads show the path of salvation to mankind. The theme of the Upanishads is to find unity in the apparent diversity before us. In one of his lectures abroad, Swamiji explained that knowledge was the finding of unity in diversity and the highest point in every science was reached when it found the one unity underlying all variety. This was true of physical science as well as spiritual.

So, what do we understand about who we really are? We are Brahman, the Impersonal God. He is without desire, not working, creating, thinking or reasoning, as all these functions lie in the domain of the human field within time, space and causation. The Impersonal God is without form and qualities and is referred to as It. It and we are One and the same. Thus, if I am the eternal Impersonal being, I am fearless, not weak, omnipotent and omnipresent and strong, "before which space melts away into nothingness" and "time vanishes into non-existence". Vedanta does not propose a God to fear, because He is our very own Self!

Finally, Swami Vivekananda says we should give up vain desires, superstitions and materialism as they are based on body consciousness. He further guides us to get out of our difficulties ourselves as we are Spirit! Give up being helpless and dependent on others and stop looking for a saviour or prophet or personal God to do everything for us. "We attribute our human characteristics, functions and limitations to God and expect him to bring us food and clothing whereas we have to do this for ourselves." "The greatest prayer is to worship the God in me, the God in you. Always look within, never without."

RAMANA MAHARISHI THE SILENT GURU

An unassuming spiritual giant, Ramana Maharishi, brought out the poetic impulse in the author and a short poem is offered as a tribute to him.

Ramana Maharishi lived at home,

All over the country he did not roam.

Many questions were answered in silence,

Seekers felt his presence evoked compliance.

He laid emphasis on direct perception,

Direct experience sought their attention.

He gained Self Realisation due to a fervent desire,

To know the reality of death.

He believed the direct, sincere and pure

Path was the best.

"Who am I" was the suggested honest quest,

Repeated to oneself internally was the best.

Discarding the five sheaths, one by one,

One reaches the Atman within, shining like the sun.

The method of self- analysis taken up each day,

Together with self-enquiry is the way.

Maharishi, the eternal guide, do bless the seekers,

May they lose their egos and follow their teachers.

A clean slate to write on was easier still,

Rather than one with deep ritualism already filled.

He suggested there was no need to superimpose

Names of Gods where Satchitananda arose.

Pure Consciousness with no name or form,

Is the Reality we must realise anon.

His direct way needs a strong personality,

To undertake the straight path, experience the Totality.

He accepted the paths of Devotion and Karma

Reached the same goal, if one followed one's Dharma.

He offered still a simple approach,

That a pure mind could follow.

Seek within and find yourself,

The external world is but hollow.

Ramana Maharishi laid emphasis on direct perception and direct experience. Having personally gained Self-realisation, brought on by an earnest and fervent desire to know the reality of death at the young age of seventeen, he saw that the direct sincere path was the best. Thus, he advised the method of self-analysis and self-enquiry as the simplest and direct way to knowing who one really is. A clean slate is easier to write on, than one already filled with ideas of a personal God and widespread ritualism. In view of this, he suggested that there was no need to superimpose names of various Gods such as Ganesh, Vishnu, Mahesh on the pure Consciousness or Satchitananda, one's real nature.

The direct method he advocated required a mature and strong personality. Though he accepted that others could take up the paths of devotion and karma and that all these paths lead to the same goal of Self-realisation, he offered a straight forward and direct path with a simple approach that a pure mind could follow.

Maharishi's responses, to questions posed to him regarding realisation of the Self (Brahman) being based on direct experience and his preference for the direct approach, are far removed from the responses of many other spiritual giants. To most queries, he replied that self-enquiry and the basic question 'who am I' when raised internally, brings about the slowing down of thoughts and quiescence of the mind, when diligently pursued. It is not a repetitive 'who am I' that is suggested by him but one main question to be placed before oneself. Subsequently the 'Not this, Not this' or' Neti, Neti' method is to be applied in order to discard the various sheaths or coverings of the individual body, from the gross to the subtle to the causal body, so that the Self, the innermost spirit can be uncovered. This will also weed out of the mind, the firm conviction presently held, that one is the body. After negating the body sheaths, the awareness remains 'That I Am'. The nature of this awareness is Existence, Consciousness and Bliss.

The Self is the real being in its natural condition, unchangeable, unmoving, permanent, pure consciousness, existence and bliss. Seeing the Self from this point of view, he declares that there is no bondage and therefore no requirement of liberation. When the Self is unattached and One alone, where would it be bound and from whom or what would it be required to be liberated? Thus sorrows, grief and unhappiness are part of the world (samsara) upto the time that one believes that one is the body. Once it is realised that one is the Self and the Self is the same as Brahman and there is only one existence which appears as the world, then bliss and only bliss abides!

Knowing one's Self is knowing God. One should never forget the Self. The Self is self-luminous and is self-manifest. The purport of meditation on the Self (Brahman) is to make the mind take the form of the Self. Therefore, one should not think of this and that, as the very thought of thinking will end in bondage. The greatest meditation is 'I am He' (Soham), the truth that one is not different from the self-luminous reality that shines like a flame. In this way one can get rid of the plurality of thoughts by meditating on this one thought. Finally, even this one thought will vanish.

All disciplines such as sacrifice, charity, jaap, puja etc are modes of meditation of the form 'I am Brahman'. One should see to it that in all these modes one does not stray away from the form 'I am Brahman'. "Reach the goal making the mind firm in the Self, through determining the nature of the real by Vedantic enquiry and by looking upon oneself and all things as of the nature of the Real." An impure mind, under the influence of Rajas and Tamas cannot experience Reality, that is subtle and unchanging. The purified mind, when it has listened to scriptures from a true guru, reflected on its meaning and meditated on Brahman, will become subtle and unmoving and will then experience that one's Self is of the nature of Brahman.

Maharishi explains that the Jiva which is mind, is in reality the pure Self. Forgetting this truth, it imagines itself to be the individual soul and gets bound in the shape of the mind. The Jiva forgets its true nature as the Self due to forgetfulness, known as the power of veiling. The veil hides the Self nature of 'I' and projects the 'I am the body' notion. In fact, the body is the cave temple where the Jiva, which is God, resides. The Jiva needs to put forth effort in the form of reflection on the Self in a gradual and sustained manner. This will destroy the mind and the notion that 'I am the body' and this state is called release. "The mind should be made to rest in the Heart till the destruction of the 'I' thought, which is of the form of ignorance residing in the heart. This itself is jnana (gyan); this alone is dhyana also". If the mind is controlled, all else can be controlled!

Realisation of the Self will be gained only when we accept that the world is unreal. What is called the world is only thought and apart from thought, there is no independent entity called the world. When there is no thought, we experience happiness and when the world appears, we go through misery. There is no lasting happiness in any object of the world. The path of knowledge, the enquiry of the form 'who am I' is the principle means to make the mind quiescent. Then this world that we see, is no longer seen. Then there is no 'I' thought, there is only Silence, the mind is resolved in the Self. The Self is the seer, the substrate, the Atman and Brahman!

In order to destroy the mind, give it a mantra to chant or take up meditation on the forms of god, as countless thoughts make each thought weak. A single one pointed and strong mind allows the self-enquiry 'who am I' to destroy other thoughts, as the mind will go back to its source. Maharishi points out that "when other thoughts arise, one should inquire 'to whom do they arise?'. When the response is 'to me', again ask 'who am I'. Repeated effort will train the mind to stay in its source, the Self, and the mind will become quiescent."

The thought 'I' is the first thought of the mind and that is ego. It is from where ego originates, that breath also originates. Therefore, when the mind becomes quiet, breath is controlled and when breath is controlled, mind becomes quiescent. Breath is the gross form of mind! It can be observed that breathing is hyperactive when one is agitated and shallow when one is feeling sad or low.

Each one is a single indivisible whole, not two, Self and ego, so when one enquires within, the ego and ignorance disappear. One knows exactly what one's true nature is through direct experience. In deep sleep or fainting despite the world disappearing one knows that 'I exist' and do not disappear.

Not seeking anything but the Self, is wisdom. Maturity of thought and enquiry alone, remove attachment to the body and enlightened enquiry leads to liberation. Renouncing the family (samsara) in the mind, is real asceticism as per Maharishi and he goes on to say that only enquiry into Brahman, should be called brahmacharya. These lofty ideals require a high level of conviction and strength which is rarely found even in the thoughts expressed by gurus worldwide.

On a query regarding prarabda which is the results of past karma interfering in one's efforts at Sadhana for enlightenment, Ramana Maharishi responded by saying that it does not interfere with internal quest, only acts when the mind is turned outward. Also, one can overcome prarabda karma in this life when the ego merges in its source, the Self. "When there is no I, there is no karma!"

The path of knowledge removes the sense of 'I' and that of devotion removes the sense of mine. In order to achieve the state of silence which is beyond thought and word, the destruction of the sense of 'I' and 'mine' is the goal. Since 'I' and 'mine' are interdependent, the end of devotion and knowledge is the same.

Dwelling in solitude (ekantvasa) is the state of being free of mental concepts and since Self is all pervasive it has no particular place for solitude. Stillness in spiritual language means cessation of thinking. "Be still and know that I am God." The simplest of quotations and yet enfolds a world of meaning wherein one must be equipped with vijnana (knowledge), the tranquil state of existence consciousness, which is like the motionless ether or waveless ocean! The act of communion with the Self (atma vyavahara) or remaining still inwardly is intense activity, which is performed with the entire mind and without break.

Action and knowledge are not obstacles to each other, as all activities take place in the realised person's presence, he as a silent witness may even be engaged in the activity but is unattached to it. Experience takes place only in the present. Beyond experience nothing exists. Past, present and future are only imagination, as space and time only exist in the mental sphere. When one goes beyond the phenomenon, space and time disappear. Shapes, forms and phenomena pass away but consciousness remains ever. The soul (Atman) does not come and go, only the thinking mind makes it appear so. The mind creates and maintains the illusion of reality as in births and deaths, till it is destroyed by Self Realisation.

Meditation on Pranav consists in reflection on the Truth of the Self. The Pranav is Omkara, consisting of three and a half 'matras'- a, u, m and ardha matra; A stands for waking state, U for dream and M for deep sleep, while ardh matra stands for Turiya state. Waking sleep (jagrat sushupti) is sleep in which there is awareness, when the mind and senses are fully alert but inactive. Just as in deep sleep, the blissful pure being prevails. Turiya is the fourth state, when the Self is the witness of the three states of waking, dream and deep sleep. This state is also called maunakshara, the silence syllable as it is present silently in all four stages and as advaita mantra being the essence of all mantras. A final stage is Turiyatita, where the awareness of all four states, all three states plus the fourth, the idea that the Self is witness, disappears. The Self is then described as Turiyatita, beyond all four, as 'IT' alone 'IS'.

Differentiating the eternal from the transient, is the practice of knowledge. While enquiry is retaining the mind in the Self, meditation is thinking that one's Self is Brahman, Existence, Consciousness, Bliss. The path of enquiry leads to Self-realisation. Other methods suggested by Maharishi to aspirants are

- Stuti – singing praises of the Lord with great devotion
- Japa – uttering name of God or Mantra mentally or verbally

- Dhyana – concentrating without contacting the objects of the senses
- Yoga – stilling the mind through breath control (pranayama)
- Jnana – annihilation of the mind through dhyana or enquiry without going back to the earlier state. Silence (mauna) and inaction refer to this state. Maya (delusion and ignorance) is completely destroyed by this intense activity called silence (mauna).

Brahman cannot be apprehended by the impure mind but can be, by the pure mind. Thus, the way shown by the Maharishi is through self-analysis and self-enquiry, only after attempting purity in mind through the eight limbs of yoga and the eight limbs of knowledge (jnana ashtanga) as specified by him. They are explained below:

Limbs of yoga.

1. Yama: cultivation of principles of good conduct
2. Niyama: observance of rules of good conduct
3. Asana: observance of different postures e.g., siddha
4. Pranayama: exhaling vital air (rechaka), inhaling (puraka) and retaining in the heart (kumbhaka)
5. Pratyahara: preventing the mind from flowing towards external names and forms through meditating on the Pranav, fixing attention between eyebrows, looking at tip of the nose or reflection on nada.
6. Dharana: fixing the mind on a locus fit for meditation, such as Heart or Brahmarandhara (aperture in the crown of the head). Think that here there shines like a flame the Self (Brahman) and fix the mind therein and meditate.

7. Dhyana: meditation through the 'I am He' thought.

8. Samadhi: after above meditation one no longer thinks that 'I am such and such' and 'I am doing this and that'. Thus the 'I' thought disappears in Samadhi. Daily practice, without falling asleep, will result in the supreme state of quiescence of the mind.

The eight limbs of knowledge (jnana ashtanga)

1. Yama: controlling sense organs, realising defects in the world e.g., the body

2. Niyama: mental concentration on the Self and Supreme Self

3. Asana: with its help constant meditation is made possible with ease

4. Pranayama: rechaka- removing name and form from object, paraka- grasping existence, consciousness, bliss and kumbhaka- retaining those aspects thus grasped

5. Pratyahara: preventing name and form from re-entering the mind

6. Dharana: keeping the mind in the heart, not letting it stray outward and realising that one is the Self itself, which is existence, consciousness, bliss

7. Dhyana: after leaving aside the body consisting of the five sheaths, one enquires 'who am I' and then one stays as the 'I' which is the Self. This is the meditation on 'I am only pure consciousness'

8. Samadhi: is when the 'I' manifestation also ceases and there is subtle, direct experience.

He clarifies that the limbs of knowledge may be practised "at all places and at all times".

Ramana Maharishi spoke less, wrote some and communicated through silence most of the time when approached. It is no doubt that the ultimate doctrine and the supreme and most direct path proposed by Bhagwan Ramana Maharishi has not been the most popular, as for most people it seemed too austere and difficult. Let the reader decide which path is most suited to his temperament and may the blessings of Ramana Maharishi be upon him.

SWAMI CHINMAYANANDA ON MEDITATION

One of the legends in spirituality was Swami Chinmayananda, here is an ode to the lofty personality, by the author.

Who can rise to your majestic height,

In physicality or spiritual might?

The snow –clad mountains of Himalayas,

Are a testimony to your endeavours.

The legacy that you left behind,

In printed books and CDs, I find.

The masters, disciples and followers galore,

Enrich the lives of others for sure.

O Swami Chinmayananda, spiritual leader of our times,

You were one above the rest in seeking the divine.

A true guru of head and heart,

Brahman you within did find.

The dust of your feet is lost to us,

Your blessings in every book reside.

May they take us on the Path,

Your light shine ahead in the dark.

The subtle art of taming the mind to forget its haunting dream visions of the world, is the art of meditation. The practice of meditation is one technique for reaching spiritual fulfilment. Once one has gained control of one's thought flow, under the discriminating intellect, one can say that one is capable of meditation. This then marks the beginning of meditation.

To begin with, let us understand a broad outline of the envelopment of the Atman within the five sheaths or coverings within the human body as specified by Vedanta.

- The Food Sheath and Air Sheath are together known as the Gross Body. The physical body, that is formed by food taken in, is called the Food Sheath, and the Air Sheath controls the faculty of perception (prana), excretion (apana), digestion (samana), circulation (vyana) and thinking (udana) when the human being is awake.

- The Mental and Intellectual Sheaths are known as the Subtle Body. The mind is light and thoughts can travel beyond the body, while the intellect being finer can spread even further to "realms unseen" in the dream state.

- The Bliss Sheath is the fifth and finest sheath, as it brings untold bliss to the human being in deep sleep, when the mind and intellect are absent. This state of non – apprehension is the Causal Body, which gives rise to the misapprehensions of the gross and subtle bodies, when the human being awakens and also when he is in the dream state.

The innermost core is the Atman. It provides the life spark to the inert human body, its organs and faculties and thereby the body, mind and intellect combine functions in its presence.

Where the mind is, the waking state and the world of cognition is. One also identifies with the mind and intellect when one looks into the world of experiences in the dream state. Withdrawing from the waking and dream state, one enters the deep sleep state and enjoys bliss. Going beyond the gross, subtle and causal bodies one identifies with the illuminating factor, the Atman in the fourth state, called by the Upanishads, the Turiya State.

In the West, philosophy is a view of life, whereas in the East, it is also a way of life. According to Vedanta, plants have basic awareness, animals more awareness, while in human beings the mind and intellect are fully developed. Beams of consciousness radiate outwards based on the purity of the mind and intellect and therefore the saint or Rishi has the maximum awareness. "To realise Pure Awareness which is Atman, or the Life Center, is the goal of life."

Swami Chinmayananda emphasised that a liberated person lies dormant in every mortal and a slight change in outlook is all that is required; viz abandon the 'I' and 'I'ness because existence as 'I' is a long eternity of pain. Since life is to seek and to discover Truth, true life can be only an eternal experiencing of the Life Divine. He suggested that one should live the Life Divine wherever one is and one need not go away to the mountains or forests. It is only essential that one is clear that "I was born only to wake up and assert my true nature, which is wisdom and bliss". The consistent practice of seeking our real identity in the Atman constitutes the Divine Life.

In Vedanta the term ignorance (avidya), nescience is explained as the self forgetfulness of one's real nature as Self, pure Consciousness. From ignorance arise desires, then thoughts and accordingly actions based on those thoughts. Only selfless, desire-less actions can lift ignorance. Where ignorance recedes, knowledge manifests. A mind controlled by intellect becomes still. A thought is not mind but a flow of thoughts is mind. Arresting the thought flow by making the mind follow a single line of thought steadily or still further reduce the flow by intensified concentration, one reaches a stage where the mind is said to be annihilated. Annihilation of the mind is the divine life to be achieved by renouncing all desires. This experience transcends both mind and intellect. It is the sublimation of our mental and intellectual Sheaths.

Swamiji lays down the guidelines for knowing oneself in order to prepare for and move on to the path of meditation for culmination in the goal of self-realisation. He says that self-evaluation is the only method of learning to know oneself. One must attend to the messy condition of our inner personality. The contrast between what we really are and what we believe ourselves to be is the most important hurdle to be crossed. Introspection or self-analysis is the cure.

Regular practice in watching one's ego with pure impartial judgement is introspection. "The observer in one becomes ashamed of the false actor within." When one observes how one pretends to be right in everything, this realisation helps in bringing about an improvement in one's personality. The best time for self analysis is at the close of each day. As soon as one apprehends a weakness in one's nature, we should substitute its opposite virtue in its place. Introspection, detection, negation and substitution are the preliminary processes in the purification of the seeker. Our daily attempts to review with detachment, our life as lived during the day, is the gateway to the path of meditation shown by Vedanta, to reach the Life Divine.

Meditation is the technique for blending our physical, mental, intellectual and spiritual aspects of our personality into one harmonious whole; in order to reach the ultimate experience of Reality.

Vedanta considers that the subtle body functions at four different levels. First, the mind operates in the field of doubts and feelings and second, the intellect as the firm discriminating and determining factor. Third the citta, the illuminating aspect that makes our thoughts apparent to us and fourth the ego, when the subtle body functions as the sense of I-ness and my-ness. Yet all four are really one. If one is transcended, the other three are also transcended. The process of meditation helps to stop the mind, transcend the intellect, crush the ego or liquidate the citta. Thus, getting established in the subtle body, one gains the necessary withdrawal from the gross body.

When we identify with the body, the ego manifests itself. The ego alone suffers pain, limitations and finally death. "Identifying with the Atman (Self), the phantom ego disappears." In its place we recognise the Divine, our true nature. Sadhana is the practice followed regularly to live a spiritual life and Purushartha is the sacred self-effort.

In order to take the first step for meditation the posture of one's body should be streamlined. The posture recommended for meditation, is to sit on a cushion or folded blanket with maximum base firmly on the seat, the vertical column erect and perpendicular to the ground. If the body is kept erect over its base it will be in equilibrium, with its centre of gravity contained in the base. The meditator must next relax the body in the elected position. By physically relaxing one's body, adjusting it into a firm neutral equilibrium, bringing breathing to a harmonious rhythm, one withdraws the attention from the outermost Gross Sheaths. The next step is to attempt to transcend consciously the Subtle Sheaths too.

It is evident that meditation is keeping the mind on one line of thinking to the complete exclusion of dissimilar thought currents. Thoughts must not be suppressed when one sits for meditation but one should stand apart as an observer and watch the procession of thoughts. There are three sources of the flood of thoughts that assail the mind: memories of the past, anxieties for the future and excitements in the present. Conscious thoughts are fully realised, whereas in the sub -conscious mind are thoughts that had met with conflict and therefore surface during dreams. In the unconscious mind lie thoughts or rather vasanas, that are deeply imbedded and come up during stress. In order to exercise control over the thoughts so that one becomes calm and is prepared for meditation, one needs to change the quality, quantity and direction of thoughts. Vedanta offers the following pathsthrough which one can change the:

- quality of thoughts through devotion (Bhakti Marg)
- quantity of thoughts through dedicated action (Karma Marg)
- direction of thoughts through knowledge (Gyan Marg).

All these paths are not mutually exclusive and need to be practised in synthesis.

In addition, Swami Chinmayananda here strongly suggests the chanting of a mantra. Chanting (Jaap) trains the mind to a single line of thinking and can bring about sustained single pointedness. There is a close connection between name and form, if one says the word 'table' one can immediately see a table before one's eyes and this is the under lying principle behind Jaap yoga. The technique to be followed is to give up the motive of profit and surrender offering pure devotion, to discover the essence of the mantra chosen by one for Jaap. One may begin chanting loudly at first before a chosen symbol, thereby involving eyes, ears and tongue. Followed by mental chanting, slowly stopping the movement of the tongue as well as the rising of the mantra in the throat. In this way, finally only the mind is chanting. Next, identifying with one's intellect, the mind can be observed to be chanting steadily. This gives rise to peace within one. Now stop the mind from chanting. The ensuing silence is a state of transcendence of the mind and intellect!

When one is completely and totally in this state of silence, one is in the realm of Truth. However, as one is not accustomed to this inner silence, one does not acknowledge it for what it is. One does not feel the consummate satisfaction of the experience because one does not know "This is That". With knowledge (Gyan) this experience begins to give us the joy that it actually contains. Otherwise, this moment of silence or "Zero Point" may be taken as a void. Knowing that this special moment is pregnant with possibilities, one would come to experience little by little, the real nature of the Self (Brahman). The final peak of success aimed at by a mind in meditation, is its own merger into the great silence- into pure Consciousness.

In case the mantra chosen for Jaap is the Gayatri Mantra, one needs to be aware that one is praying for spiritual unfoldment. This mantra is an invocation to the Lord Sun. In our inner life the sun represents the illuminator of all our experiences, the Atman.

Om, the most powerful single syllable mantra is accepted as being one with Brahman and also the medium that connects the human being to God (Brahman). Om (AUM) represents the Self (Atman) in all four stages of existence that is, waking (A), dream (U), deep sleep (M) and silence (Turiya). The sounds A, U and M are called Matras and the silence, the common principle that pervades them all is called Amatra-Om. A single common factor that pervades the three stages of waking, dream and deep sleep and is yet not conditioned by any of them while being a witness is the silence, Turiya, the real changeless intelligent principle. Thus, AUM plus Turiya together comprise the totality of the manifestation of Atman- Brahman.

As per Swami Chinmayananda, "Vedanta promotes the growth and happiness of the human being both in his individual and communal life and points a way to reach the Beyond but surely in and through life." Progress is not possible without renunciation. To climb a ladder, one needs to leave the lower rung to get on to the next higher one and therefore give up false values and acquire higher ones. Live the right values and with such "integrity of character", "meditate and grow".

SWAMI TEJOMAYANANDA ON HOW TO LIVE BY VEDANTA

Swami Tejomayananda was a student of Swami Chinmayananda, who had founded Chinmaya Mission worldwide. Now, as head of the mission, he provides courses and discourses on all spiritual topics related to Vedanta, as well as the practical application thereof in everyday life. Beneath the apparent simplicity and humility of character displayed by him, lies a strong conviction in the principles of Vedanta, that find expression in the commentaries he has written and many original compositions he has authored on Vedanta and Bhakti, thereby carrying forward the tradition laid down by Swami Chinmayananda.

Some of his thoughts are expressed here. Vedanta is a means of knowledge, that **reveals an object as it truly is**. Thus, Vedanta reveals even our true nature. The finite knower ceases and realises his infinite nature and once one becomes aware that our true nature is bliss, one stops looking outward for means of happiness. It teaches us about who we are, the nature of the world and God. This enables us to interact suitably with all beings and God. This knowledge can be experienced and verified directly by anyone who has a pure mind. Even an illiterate person can gain the supreme Truth.

Swamiji goes on to explain the various aspects of the body that we normally identify with as 'I' and which according to Vedanta are not the real 'I', such as body, mind, intellect and ego. The body is therefore experienced as 'mine' and not as I.

The mind is an instrument of thinking, a flow of thoughts, a doer of actions and the instrument of experiences, be they joyful or sorrowful. When the mind is attached to sense objects, it causes bondage. When it is absorbed in thoughts of God, the same mind leads one to liberation and freedom, peace and fulfilment.

Intellect helps us take decisions in life on ordinary matters, as well as on subtler, spiritual matters where vivek (discrimination) is required, such as freedom from the bondage of worldly desires.

Ego is the notion of individuality, that arises when we identify with something. It takes on new forms and gives up old forms all the time, whilst itself remaining formless, for example, I am a teacher or I am fat. But, as Ramana Maharishi says "it disappears like a ghost when enquired into". The ego identifies with the body, mind, intellect and their characteristics and also with their activity, giving rise to the notion of doership. This doership binds him to the results of the actions and thus he goes on to enjoy or suffer them, as the case may be.

Results of actions leave impressions (vasanas) on the mind, which in turn prompt actions. This cycle continues till one realises that one is only playing a role and is not the actual doer. Actions done without ego, selfishness, likes and dislikes, do not bind. Actions can be offered to the Self within and when thus carried out will not bind, as one is the instrument of the Atman within. A beautiful statement quoted by Swamiji clarifies this succinctly: "The flute makes itself hollow free of all ego and pride and allows the Flute- bearer to play His divine music through it".

Now once it is accepted that one is not the body, mind, intellect and ego, it is still to be determined as to who one is.

In all one's worldly experiences, it is seen that the term 'I am' is always present. One cannot experience one's own absence. One exists and therefore everything else exists. One is conscious (aware) that I am. I am the eternal, infinite Existence. The knower is Consciousness and the known is inert. The knower illumines the body, mind, intellect and the experiences. Therefore, the knower is the infinite Self that has a body, mind, intellect combine. The body is no longer 'I' but 'mine'.

Brahman is the very knowledge principle or Consciousness because of which all thoughts, feelings and objects are known. Brahman is the sentient factor, without which no action is possible. All actions happen in its presence alone. Just as the ocean controls the waves from within and without; so also, the Self guides us, as our conscience from within and through the laws of nature from without. Brahman and nature are impartial to all beings providing rain, sunshine and even devastation through floods and earthquakes to all equally!

Vedanta clearly defines that the world emerges from, remains in and merges back into Truth (Brahman) and that the world is not a modification of Brahman but is a superimposed appearance on It. The superimposition does not have a separate existence from the substratum. They are essentially one. The world has no existence other than Brahman and is in essence Brahman alone. The world is the snake and Brahman the rope in the snake, superimposed on the rope in the example. Since the world is in essence Brahman and "I", the infinite Self, am Brahman, the world is not different from me.

Swami Tejomayananda specifies that knowledge should be acquired through the right means of knowledge, be it direct perception, inference or verbal testimony. He also says that attachment is the weakness of the mind and confusion, indecision, dullness and doubt are faults of intellect. In order to overcome them the intellect should decide on matters of Dharma or duty through the Dharma Shastras e.g Vedas or Shrutis and about spiritual matters through Vedanta. In order to realise Truth, the study of Vedanta with deep commitment and regular practice, needs to be taken up. Spiritual practices, such as worship (puja) and repetition of God's name or a mantra (jaap) help purify the mind. Listening to scriptures (shravana) and reflection on them (manana) and meditation or contemplation on such knowledge (nididhyasana), strengthen spiritual knowledge for the student or person on the spiritual path.

Swamiji says "practice of Vedanta does not mean any physical action, like pranayama. It is to remind ourselves time and again to live a conscious and alert life, with the vision of Vedanta". Whenever one is sad or feeling low, one should assert "I am Bliss Absolute" and one will feel strengthened. In this way, a pure, concentrated and subtle mind easily abides in the Truth (Brahman) and Living Vedanta becomes easy and joyous.

Section IV

AN INSIGHT INTO THE UPANISHADS

KATHOPANISHAD

In order to bring the young lad of this Katha (story) before us, a poem coined by the author follows.

Naciketas a young boy of nine,

Well versed in Shastras he did shine.

Lord of Death he sought out,

To help clear his pressing doubt.

Is there life after death?

Or is all over with the breath?

Yama offered him riches and progeny,

Admonishing him not to seek this mystery.

Naciketas with discrimination asserted,

When death will ensue, what use he blurted.

Tell me the Truth, the Reality behind,

This life shall end, what will I find?

Finding him to be a true disciple,

Yama told him birth and death is a cycle.

Embrace the good, ignore the pleasurable,

The goal is your inner Self that is attainable.

Aum is the Self and the Reality,

The Atman and Brahman and Totality.

Sadhna and meditation will take you forward,

Concentration, single- pointedness lead you onward.

Adhyatma yoga learnt from the guru,

Brings one to Brahman, if one is pure and true.

Past, present, future parts of time,

Disappear in the spiritual clime.

Naciketas a young boy of nine,

Realised Truth and went beyond Time.

Introducing us to Kathopanishad, Sadguru Sri Swami Tapovanji apprises us that Kathopanishad is one of the ten classic Upanishads that explains Brahma- vidya or Atman-vidya, the knowledge of Brahman or Atman. This knowledge destroys ignorance and reveals that Atman which is eternal bliss, is within one's body and is one's own Self. Listening to discourses on this Upanishad and studying it provides intellectual knowledge, but realising the Self in its eternal luminous nature requires a calm, pure, concentrated and controlled mind. Renunciation (vairagya) and meditation on the Atman by such an individual will lead to the blissful experience of Atman within us. In order to ensure that one remains in this blissful state, the path suggested by Swamiji is to control the five senses and mind, make the intellect steady and then practise upasana through jaap and meditation on the form and qualities of a personal god, so as to make the mind totally pure.

Naciketas, the young hero of this Upanishad was empowered with total vairagya and thus he unhesitatingly refused all the luxuries offered to him by Lord Yama, the lord of death and insisted on being told about the truth beyond death. He thus mastered the teachings of Brahma- vidya taught to him by Yama and undertaking yoga similar to that outlined by Swami Tapovanji above, he meditated and realised the Self, Atman. To all students and aspirants Swamiji's advice is to "strive to become and be".

A little background before the discussion between Nacikatas and Yama, the lord of death will help us in understanding the high spiritual level at which this interaction takes place. Naciketas, a young Brahmin boy of nine years, was astonished when he saw his father distribute barren cows as part of a Visvajit Yagna to the priests assembled at their house. He was also aware that this sacrifice is only fulfilled when one gives away all one has, as he was well versed in the Shastras (religious texts). He therefore asked his father "to whom wilt thou give me?" Angered by his question uttered a third time, his father retorted, "unto death do I give thee". The intelligent young boy wondered what mission would be fulfilled by Lord Death (Yama) through him.

Naciketas then arrived at the gates of Yama's palace only to find Yama was away and would return after three days. The boy waited without food and drink and when Yama discovered his guest had not eaten for three days, he apologised to him and granted him three boons. For the first boon Naciketas asked that his father may forget his anger towards him, sleep peacefully and welcome him with affection when he returns. For the second boon he asked Lord Death to teach him the Fire sacrifice that mortals want to learn in order to enjoy the pleasures of heaven, which they consider immortality. When Naciketas learns it perfectly, Yama is very pleased and names the ritual Naciketas Fire Sacrifice from then on. Naciketas has used the first boon for his father and the second for human beings on earth. The third boon takes us to the Supreme Self, Brahman. He asks lord Death to tell him if there is life after death.

Yama offers him riches, long life and progeny instead of the answer to Naciketas' question, but Naciketas is adamant that he has no use for worldly goods, as after all, in the end death will ensue. A self-realised person is the best guru (teacher) for a disciple perfected through inner purification. The disciple gains complete knowledge of Brahmavidya instantaneously, when such a guru explains it to him. Due to his discrimination and detachment, Naciketas refuses even the "subtlest of joys" of Brahmalok, where one exhausts one's good karma.

Having found Naciketas to be a worthy student, Yama begins his teaching by telling him of the two options of the good and pleasurable that a human being is offered time and again in life. The good option helps the individual to grow in spirituality and character, while the pleasurable one gives temporary enjoyment in the phenomenal world. Knowledge and ignorance too, lead to different fruits, while knowledge provides one with light and understanding the goal of liberation and enlightenment; ignorance keeps one in darkness and engrossed in the wicked ways of life, believing that this life is all there is. Thus, those who follow the path of ignorance and pleasure become slaves to death and continue in the cycle of birth and death and birth again.

Yama then goes on to explain meditation, through which one gains Self Perfection. A purified, highly concentrated mind is brought to contemplate on the nature of the Self exclusively. Subtlety is measured as pervasiveness and Atman being the subtlest among body, prana, mind and intellect is imagined as bliss lying in the innermost recesses of the human being, A combination of pure mind and pure intellect, freed from all negativity and with thoughts withdrawn from external objects, meditates on the inner Atman and "recognises the Ancient" Self as the Truth. This technique of communion with the Atman is known as Adhyatma Yoga.

Naciketas now asks his guru to expound on the nature of Reality. His enquiry points out to Truth that lies beyond virtue and vice, which is neither the cause nor the effect and which does not belong to the past or to the future. Here virtue and vice represent all pairs of opposites. Since Reality or Atman is One, it cannot be limited by another and therefore no pairs of opposites exist in it. It is beyond qualities and is the witness, pure consciousness, awareness, eternal and immortal!

As regards cause and effect, the Atman seems as if it is the uncaused cause and is not involved in the unending logic of what caused this cause. Thus, the Atman is the Principle, which is neither the cause nor the effect.

Leaving aside memories of the past and anxieties of the future, Naciketas wants to know the Eternal Reality that is beyond Time. In response to this Yama said that, Om is the goal pointed out by all the Upanishads. It is also the Pratika (idol of Brahman) for purpose of worship and for meditation with form. "Om is verily Brahman alone" proclaims the Kathopanishad. Here in this mantra 16 of valli 2, it is clearly stated that Om is the Reality itself. A follower of Vedanta can meditate on Om, to reach either the Sagun Brahman (with form) or Nirgun Brahman (without form). Also, he can gain Brahmalok, if he so desires, or if he desires the Ultimate Reality, he can become "That"! Yama says that the Eternal Ultimate Reality is fully symbolised in the word "Om"!

In an attempt to describe the Atman, a comparison with space is made. A pot made within space has space within it already. Space is not poured into the pot after it is made. Similarly, the human body is made within Atman and Atman exists within it too as the presiding deity all through birth, growth, decay, disease and death.

Vyasa has taken much of the philosophy of the Bhagwad Gita from this Upanishad, as is evident from the next thought as well, which goes on to express that the one who thinks "I am slain" and the one who thinks "I slay" are both in error as neither does the Atman slay nor is it slain. It is eternal, all pervading and the subtlest, hence smallest within every bit of space and is the greatest as IT envelopes and penetrates through space and is further than all the universes in and beyond space.

The seeker with a purified intellect and single pointed mind accesses a tranquil plane, that helps him realise his identity with the Atman. He goes beyond sorrow and pain, as these are attached to body, mind and intellect and as Atman he is beyond them. The Atman, all pervading Truth, is a motionless entity that cannot go anywhere as there is no spot where it is not already. The individual is described as 'sitting he goes far' and 'lying he goes everywhere' only as the mind travels to distant places as mental waves.

The pure mind alone, detached from the false through discrimination, gets attached to the Truth. Atman cannot be gained only by the study of Vedas etc but by concentrated meditation on Atman itself, then Atman reveals itself. Yama says that both the high classes and the common folk have to go through the same self-purification process to reach the Atman.

In the Kathopanishad is given a beautiful comparison of the parts of a horse drawn chariot with the body, mind, intellect and senses of the human being. The same has been adapted by the sage Vyasa in an elaborate and memorable manner in his Bhagwad Gita Upanishad. The comparisons go as such: Self is the master of the chariot, the chariot is the human body, the mind its reins, the intellect the intelligent charioteer, the horses the sense organs and the roads the sense objects. The unrestrained mind allows the senses uncontrolled access and such an impure, thoughtless being continues in the round of births and deaths without ever reaching Self Realisation. However, a pure being using his discrimination between the good and pleasant reaches the Supreme goal from "whence none is born again".

Answering Naciketas query, Yamraj says that Atman, the vital intelligence that presides over the sense organs, is by nature Knowledge Absolute. There is nothing in this world that is unknown to it. It is a dynamic presence within us which is above body consciousness. Desires arise from a sense of incompleteness and only end in giving one sorrow. Therefore, Vedanta urges us to know, experience, perceive and realise the Atman as the Supreme Self, Brahman, "This is verily That!".

The method or yoga of Meditation is practised as a slow and steady withdrawal of attention by sinking the mind in the intellect and then deeper into the Turiya state. The Upanishad goes on to exhort the sadhak to "Arise, Awake" and walk on the direct path that is like the "sharp edge of a razor" and recognise the divinity in one. Silent meditation helps one to connect with the inner Self as it is without sound, touch, form, taste, smell, decay, without beginning and end, eternal and unchanging and free from the jaws of death! Having realised the Self, the Upanishad Rishis considered the universe as an appearance created by Maya. Also, that Brahman appears as Jiva through the conditioning by Maya.

Lord of Death continues to explain that the Gyani uses the symbol Om for meditation and the householder uses the Fire for worship. The Truth worshipped by both is the same, Brahman. The five elements are considered in Vedanta as the presiding deities of the five sense organs, for example, ear by akash(space) as sound is created and conveyed only in space, light by sun as one can see only in its presence. These five elements depend on the Supreme Self for their existence as Pranas. Thus, the one Self that exists in the heart of the individual also sustains all of creation as the Universal Self. If one does not get this vision of Oneness within and without, full Self-realisation is not achieved and one continues to go through the cycle of birth and death repeatedly. "Vedantik Self Realisation, is not a mere experiencing of the true nature of our divinity alone"; but is the oneness of the inner individual Self (Atman) and the outer total Self (Brahman).

The Atman, also called the Purush here, is described as a thumb like (jyoti) light in the heart of an individual for purposes of meditation, for the early stages of practice. I recall a senior lecturer having accepted this description literally and being adamant that the Atman is a thumb like formation in the heart centre! Let us not digress, the Atman maintains the flow of energy or vital airs (pranas) in the body and keeps it functioning till death occurs. Thus, the respiratory and blood circulatory systems, digestive system, etc function in the presence of the Atman and when the Atman leaves, the vital airs perish.

There is no change in the Atman when it leaves the body at death, nor is there any movement of it. It is the Jiva, with its sense of I-ness and My-ness that moves from one body to the next. Where the Jiva goes after death is dependent on and conditioned by one's Karma and the degree of knowledge of the Reality gained during the past life.

The Atman, as Intelligence illuminates the world of the waking, dream and deep sleep states without itself undergoing any of the experiences. The Atman being itself the light of wisdom, requires no other light. "The sun does not shine here, nor does the moon, nor do the stars, nor does the lightening, much less the fire. When He shines everything shines after Him; by His light, all shine." This Atman within is the Brahman, wherein lie all the worlds. It pervades the visible and invisible worlds and also transcends them all. It is at once immanent and transcendent. The spiritual substance is the same but it takes on different forms in the world. The Atman within is the same but our forms are different according to our experiences and resultant minds.

The sages who experience through their intuitive faculty, the Reality as the One who has made "His one form manifold", alone find peace. In moments of deep meditation, his awareness comes to be aware of itself as the Self, or in other words, one's consciousness becomes conscious of itself as Pure Consciousness. This is the moment of Self Realisation. This "Self-awareness of the Self", "This is That" says Lord Yama to Naciketas. Such poetic statements lift one to a sublime and lofty plane!

A very interesting feature is brought out at the beginning of the sixth chapter of Kathopanishad (valli 6), of the fact of vibrating matter elements with the constant Pure Intelligence as its axis. An everyday example helps illustrate this. When the josh stick (agarbatti) is rotated fast on its axis, a golden circle appears which is formed by its glowing tips, but in fact does not exist! Similarly, when matter vibrates in Prana, which is the energy of Brahman, at great speed, it gives the appearance of solid forms such as the objects of the world around us. We are aware that physicists have discovered that atom is made up of electrons and protons moving at high speed around a motionless neutron. Thus, matter is nothing but vibrating energy has been scientifically proved now, but this was known in the Vedic ages too! Once one realises that the source of all life and existence is the Vital Factor, Brahman that exists within us, one attains immortality!

Another famous concept of the Ashwatha (pipal) tree being compared to the phenomenal world mentioned in this Upanishad has been adopted by Sage Vyas in the Bhagwad Gita. The tree is described as inverted with its roots upwards in Brahman, from which it gets its nourishment and sustenance, and yet the changeable tree can be cut with the power of discrimination, such a contradictory fact is realised that it is but temporary as compared to its source, Brahman the permanent and unchangeable!

It is emphasised again that only the human being has the divine freedom with his sensitive, intuitive mind to hasten his own evolution, to realise the Self within this lifetime. Intuition is here beautifully delineated as the capacity to know Knowledge or Self. Intuition is developed when first the mind is silent and then the intellect dies in the resultant peace, leaving behind a power called intuition.

When looking at oneself in the mirror, one recognises oneself, not the image. Thus, when the evolved person comes face to face with the eternal self through intuitive knowledge, the reflection merges with the Self and one recognises that one is not the reflection but the Eternal Self.

Naciketas by imbibing the teachings of his revered guru, Yama, the Lord of Death, practised Brahma Vidya in solitude and gained Self Realisation.

MANDUKYA UPANISHAD

The theme of the Mandukya Upanishad being AUM, a descriptive poem on AUM composed by the author begins this chapter.

Vaisvanara, Vishwa the day is here,

Mind and intellect do appear.

A is the first letter of Aum,

Awake, arise, Upanishad calls one home.

Gross bodies enact cause and effect,

Emotions, actions express the rest.

Taijas, the letter U does dream world bring,

Mind and intellect once again swing.

Superior I am to you- U to A,

From your waking world I come to stay.

Cause and effect are alive here too,

Sorrow, hatred, anger they woo.

Prajna M is the deep sleep state,

'I do not know' is his take.

Waking and dream roll into me,

Mind and intellect set me free.

Ignorance emits the causal plane,

In bliss my body remains sane.

Turiya slowly ascendency gains,

Silence emerges and destroys pains.

The three that went before,

Superimposed on Turiya are.

Silence between two consecutive Aums,

Is the Turiya that in splendour roams.

Turiya is Aum, Atman is Aum,

Brahman is Aum, Self is Aum.

May Aum lead one to Reality,

Experience Oneness, merge in Totality.

One of the shortest and most poignant Upanishads, with only twelve Shlokas, is the Mandukya Upanishad. The best example of brevity in style, words and shlokas with a depth of meaning, this Upanishad also lends itself to succinct explanation of the Supreme Reality, Atman. Since Aum is the spiritual shabd (word) accepted here to represent Atman and Brahman and a world of knowledge is contained in the twelve shlokas, a study of the Karika written by Sri Gaudapada, the revered guru of Shankaracharya allows one to gain complete clarity in understanding the Upanishad.

A quaint meaning of the title lies in the name Mandukya, which means frog and we know that it hibernates under wet mud for approximately nine to ten months. The frog emerges in the rainy season to croak its message to anyone who will listen. Similar is the pattern followed by the wise man, who meditates in seclusion for a long period and then comes forth to share his Knowledge of Self-Realisation with the world!

Now let us move on to see how Atman or Aum is divided into three plus one or four parts. The first is the waking stage called Vaisvanara or Viswa represented by the letter 'A' of Aum. The vital breath (prana), mind, intellect, together with sense organs of knowledge and actions, ego and chit are all active in this state and are the nineteen mouths that bring awareness of the phenomenal world through thoughts and feelings. We undertake actions as reactions and responses to stimuli received. The seven limbs of the cosmos and correspondingly of the individual are (1) effulgent region- the head, (2) the sun- eyes, (3) air- vital breath, (4) space- middle part of body, (5) water- kidney, (6) earth- feet, (7) fire- mouth. This description reminds us of the Viswa or Virat Roop of Lord Krishna in Bhagwad Gita.

The second part is the dream state expressed by the letter 'U' of Aum and known as Taijas. Here the nineteen mouths and seven limbs of the individual are active but here it is the mental plane. This stage seems as real as the waking stage, as during it one feels pain or joy, heat or cold, similar to the waking state. In both stages the mind and intellect are active and duality prevails. In Viswa the mind and intellect are identified with the gross body and external world, in Taijasa one is identified with the subtle body and the mental world.

The third part is the deep sleep stage known as Prajna and expressed by the letter 'M' of Aum, where the mind and intellect are absent. Since the mind is the creator of agitations and these are absent too, this deep sleep stage is considered the state of bliss. Here while the rest of the nineteen mouths and seven limbs are inactive, the pranas are functioning in the presence of the spiritual centre and keep the body alive.

Though one is a homogeneous mass of consciousness and awareness, but due to the absence of the mind, intellect and ego one has no knowledge and is thus called Avidya or ignorance and is a condition of 'I do not know', Vedanta says here the Atman is identified with the causal body. This is a period of inactivity and rest. No agitations, no desires and thus no sorrows as one is neither awake nor dreaming. In fact, Prajna the blissful state, Anandmayi is the gateway to the waking and dream states which emerge from its restful condition to one of external and mental activity.

The deep sleep stage, of no knowledge, has within it the light that illumines all and is pregnant with pure consciousness, which is the controller of all, from which everything emerges and merges back into.

The possibility of reaching this pure consciousness is expressed in an extremely subtle and poetic manner. Just as a prism disperses light thrown on it in various directions and in various hues, so also the mind and intellect, when active, show the self or Atman as the various forms, names and colours of the external and mental world. These in both cases are distortions and far from the truth.

Thus, in the absence of the prism like mind, if one is able to transcend all the first three stages of waking, dream and deep sleep, one could reach the Turiya or fourth stage, the reality of Aum, Brahman or Atman. How so? Transcend or go beyond mind and intellect and allow the awareness projected by one to merge with the pure consciousness ever present around one, so that one comes to realise the Truth or Reality in the names and forms. This Truth, Reality, Atman or Pure Consciousness is the One Principle behind all three stages or quarters of Aum.

Poetic sublime levels and philosophical heights are reached in the expression of the **fourth quarter of Aum known as Turiya.** Turiya is Atman itself and the Upanishad is emphatic that the Atman is to be realised! Since it is neither conscious of the external world nor of the internal world, is not a mass of consciousness, is not simple consciousness and finally is not even sub-consciousness, then what is it? it is peaceful, auspicious and non-dual, the Self, Turiya or Atman. The only pointers are through negation of all the things that we can think of or perceive or indeed feel. **It being the subject itself,** it cannot be cognised by the sense organs, mind or intellect.

Turiya is not the waker, dreamer or deep sleeper and is not even conscious of the in between state of waking and dream where one is a little aware of both states. It is not insentient and does not have form and has no relationship with anything. There is no sign from which one can infer its reality. True then it is indescribable, as the negation of all phenomena known to one leads to Turiya, as One alone, where duality cannot enter. **It is thus of the nature of Conscience, Pure consciousness, Pure Knowledge, Pure Bliss, Peace and Auspiciousness. This Truth is to be meditated upon in order to reach actual realisation of Turiya, Atman, Brahman and Self.**

Having understood how the ego experiences the three states of Vaisnavara, Taijasa and Prajna as superimposed on the three syllables of Aum, 'A' the waking, 'U' the dream, 'M' the deep sleep states, in the gross, subtle and causal bodies and having gained theoretical knowledge of the fourth state, Turiya which is the sum total of Aum; one now approaches the **Aum mantra** to see what it signifies as sound.

For the sound limbs of Aum, one begins with the Vaisnavara or Viswa 'A' sound which is the very fundamental of all sounds, as on opening one's mouth 'a' is the first sound produced. Also, in the three ego experiences, the waking state is the very first linked to the letter 'A'. The all pervasiveness of the letter 'A' is easily established by the fact that 'a' sound is in all sounds. Again, the waking state "pervades the entire universe". The Upanishad declares that one who 'knows', has identified the waking state ego with such an 'A' alphabet of Aum, gains all desires and becomes a prominent citizen in his lifetime.

Taijasa or letter 'U' comes after 'A' and is therefore considered superior. Also, the contents of the dream state are based on the experiences of the waking state, hence superior again. Another comparison is that 'U' comes between 'A' and 'M' and the dream state comes between waking and deep sleep states. Thus, a meditator on such a 'U' sound in Aum chanting, develops an extraordinary perfection in mind and intellect.

Prajna, the last letter 'M' in Aum, is related to the deep sleep state of mass consciousness. Consciousness in the form of waking and dream folds into deep sleep to rest there without activity. Similarly, when Aum is uttered 'A' and 'U' roll into and merge in 'M'. When Aum is chanted again, 'A' and 'U' sounds seem to emerge out of 'M'. Likewise, the waking and dream states seem to emerge out of the deep sleep state rejuvenated after their rest. 'M' and deep sleep state also ensure that the plurality and the differences that were manifested in the waking and dream states disappear and merge to become one homogeneous mass of consciousness. The Upanishad declares that this stage of Prajna, can be compared to a measuring glass, as it takes all within it and gives it out when the time comes in equal measure. A meditator on this identity of Prajna attains expert understanding and discrimination.

The Mandukya Upanishad now takes one to an amazing experience, when the mantra Aum is chanted with full awareness, it lends itself to a surprising discovery of a silence between two consecutive Aums! This silence is Turiya. This is Atman. This is the eternal One, Brahman, Pure Consciousness, Bliss, Knowledge and Truth. This, the fourth state of Turiya, eternal and immortal, Knowledge absolute and in essence bliss, is superimposed upon by the three states of Vaisnavara, Taijasa and Prajna. During meditation the intent is to find in the three letters of Aum the three stages just mentioned as three distinct personalities in us. Finally, the silence of Aum is to be realised as the goal as Turiya, Atman, Brahman, Aum.

In that silence the sense organs cannot function and so the mind cannot comprehend it. This soundless Aum "is to be considered as the experience of the Turiya". There are no material gains from meditating on the soundless Aum, but the "meditator becomes what he meditates upon". Meditating regularly on the silent aspect of Aum, one gets merged into the experience of the Eternal Atman, dropping the egoistic superimpositions of separateness on the way. Trying to catch and hold onto the silence between two consecutive Aums, the mind and intellect become single-pointed and steady. One rises to the level where time no longer exists and one can take the leap to the Eternal and become one with it. This intention fructifies in the ultimate experience of realising oneself as Omniscient and Omnipresent. "The Infinite and the Eternal is not there and some other time. It is here and now!"

The disciple must go deep into the silence and remain there as long as he can. If Aum is chanted as frequently as one asserts "I am", the mind would be unified with Aum and since Aum is Brahman, one would experience Brahman itself. Aum vibration and experiencing the meaning of Aum in its totality makes one lose one's fear, a mental disturbance that covers agitations, desires and passions.

Aum, the Pranav is the substratum on which life play acts and is the symbol of Brahman behind creation, sustenance and dissolution of the phenomenal world. Knowing Aum is 'knowing' or becoming Brahman. In Vedanta the term 'knowing', or 'to know' means 'becoming', or 'to realise the Self'. In the Karika of this Upanishad, Gaudapada expresses that Aum is Ishwara, the Lord ever present in the hearts of all and that he is all pervading. A picture of Lord Krishna in the Bhagwad Gita rises uncontrollably in the mind! Understanding Omkara in its full significance of Aum as the sound, silence, waking, dreaming, deep sleep conditions, substratum, Ishwara, nirguna and saguna (with and without form), all pervading, within and without, beyond time, space and causation, as Vaisnavara, Taijasa, Prajna and Turiya, one realises the Self, Atman, Brahman and Aum!

It is important to see how cause and effect function within the waking and dream stages. Reality or pure knowledge being a stable, calm, unmoving, peaceful and blissful condition, does not lend itself to any activity. It is ignorance or avidya that becomes the cause in our waking condition and it causes activities, feelings and thoughts, which in turn result in effects. Thus, effect is inherent in the cause. The waking and dream states are both affected by cause and effect. In ignorance of our eternal and real nature, one has projected oneself into the delusional external and mental world and live tormented, due to actions and reactions undertaken as a result of cause and effect, in the external world of objects. Prajna or deep sleep is affected by cause alone as one experiences ignorance alone or 'I do not know' in this state, as it is the state of non-apprehension of reality! Turiya on the other hand, being Reality, itself is Pure Knowledge. Viswa, Taijasa and Prajna are superimpositions on it. Thus, the non-apprehension of Reality is the cause and the misapprehension of the waking and dream states are the effect. Transcending both cause and effect, one experiences Reality in the 'fourth plane of Consciousness', the Turiya.

To sum up, when ignorance disappears the cause too vanishes and then the effects cannot remain, thus the external and internal worlds also disappear. On the awakening of the Atman, the illusion of duality and plurality created by Maya vanishes and the famous call of the Upanishads to Awake, Arise and experience the Truth as it really is, shakes the very foundations of the illusory waking, dream and deep sleep consciousness and one reaches the realm of Turiya Consciousness.

KENOPANISHAD

Kenopanishad enquires into the nature of Reality or Brahman. Since the Upanishads cannot and do not answer directly as to what Brahman is, a suggestive manner and indicative meaning is used to explain its nature, as also the preconditions for experiencing Reality. The author has penned a few lines in this context and they are placed below for your perusal.

Living in constant fear of the other,

Efforts continue to please and placate another.

Incompleteness assails the temperament,

Fulfilment alone can contain the predicament.

Reality I seek thee earnestly,

You dwell within, but evade discovery.

Ego mine, reality does hide,

Clouds readily raise the tide.

Essence of ornaments lies in gold,

Tattva of human beings is in the soul.

Universal Oneness is the Truth Principle,

Brahman the Reality is, oh so simple.

Superimposition of ego has distorted,

Pure consciousness into name, form resorted.

Vedanta bring the Truth before me,

 Maya lift the veil over Reality.

Vedanta replies mind, intellect and speech,

Without purity Reality cannot reach.

Self-restraint, self-effort and lack of pride,

Take one to Self-realisation in this very life.

The Sanskrit language was most suited to this purpose and was adopted in the Upanishads to disclose the road "to the within'. The Truth discussed in the Vedas is eternal, though the books themselves may get destroyed, the theme or Truth contained in them will never be destroyed.

When one tries to understand Reality, the first and most formidable roadblock one faces is the ego, the familiar identity one has lived with, which answers every time one raises the word 'I'. This ego is in fact unsubstantial, a myth and a "shadow- nothingness", that is responsible for one's mortality and sorrow. In ignorance the ego has been superimposed on one's Reality. It lives in memories and in anxieties and hopes of the future and ends only when one experiences Reality.

What then is this Reality? It is the essence of: mud of which a large number of mud idols are made; cotton of which many threads, designs, patterns and cloth are made; gold of which a variety of gold ornaments are made; the ocean from which waves, bubbles and froth are made and finally the spirit from which a variety of human beings, animals and plants are projected forth.

Now when everything emerges from its essence and merges back into its source, there is ultimately the one alone that exists, as the "Universal Oneness is the Truth Principle". Names change with the forms but the basic, fundamental Truth remains the same. So, from the standpoint of Truth there is no plurality or difference. Realising my real nature as I am God, as there is only One. As long as I am the ego there are two, ego and God.

The next answer one seeks is, where this world has come from and has God created it. Vedanta gives a clear response here that not only the world, but the ego too, seem to exist due to the veiling power of Maya. The superimposition of the ego on the individual Reality, as well as the world on Brahman; together with the misapprehension of the rope, as a snake in the dark, create illusions and delusions such as a mirage full of water in a dry desert. Vedanta states that the Reality does not and cannot change.

What are some of the prerequisites for experiencing Reality? Purushartha, self-effort is the most important criterion, followed by self-improvement through character strengthening. Starting with identifying one's weaknesses and replacing them with positive values, one improves one's personality and character and strengthens oneself to take up the path of realising the Truth.

Prarbdha, which is preordained due to our past actions, thoughts and experiences, being the effect of earlier created causes, controls the present and future to some extent. Cause is that which was and effect is that which is. The past causes the present and the present will cause the future. The present can be modified by human intelligence to provide a better (or worse) future by self-effort, Purushartha.

Human beings are allowed a limited freedom by the law of Karma, due to their reasoning capacity and discriminative faculty. The plant and animal species are guided by their natural instincts and impulses alone. Humans are also provided the opportunity of gaining Self Realisation, through self-improvement, with the help of devotion, vivek, vairagya, discrimination, detachment from the false and mumuksutva-burning desire for Self-Realisation. While destiny brings before one fields (lokas) based on one's past, Karma makes one the architect for one's own future.

Kenopanishad like other Upanishads, is also a discussion between the Shishya (student) and the Guru (teacher) on the most secret and intimate knowledge of Reality. The student's first question is "what is the dynamic, vital force behind the mind that makes it vibrant with life and activity?" or "directed by whom does the mind run out through the senses?" Sense organs, mind and intellect are made up of insentient matter, so how can inert matter act and since it is seen to act, what makes it active?

The theory of perception in Vedanta is that the "Atman Caitanya" riding the mind, flows out through the sense organs to the sense object and the mind takes the form of the object and this reaches the intellect. The intellect then processes it based on past knowledge and memory and the person cognises it. The student, based on this theory, raises the query "directed by whom does the mind run out?" The seeker is aware that the eyes cannot see on their own and there has to be a very subtle power behind the eye instrument that empowers it. The student is obviously a perfect seeker and the Upanishad through the perfect Guru, must point out the Atman within as the divine spark that allows the mind and intellect to function as if alive, in its presence.

One needs a very pure mind and intellect to dive into the depths of Reality and this can be achieved by analysing one's thoughts and motives. Such a search within, with sincere Sadhana, will bring an external guru required at that stage, as per the law of spirituality and this is as confirmed by Vedanta. Ultimately the guru- shishya discussion moves within one, to resolve the confusions in the mind with a purified mind and intellect. The mind is the disciple and the intellect the guru.

So far, we have looked at the student's query in much detail. Now let us understand the teacher's response. The teacher replies "it is the ear of the ear, the mind of the mind and also similarly the tongue, life and eye. He goes on to say that having given up the sense of self and I- ness in these and thus rising above sense life, the wise become immortal. The suggestive response indicates undoubtedly that the sense organs, mind and intellect are incapable of functioning on their own but require a power within. This power is the Atman within, but it is not expressly stated here. The teacher is indicating that the student must prepare himself to enter the world of Truth, where Truth will be found not by the senses, nor understood or known by the intellect, as Truth is itself the seer and knower.

Truth can be known only by one's own spiritual perception or developed intuition. The teacher can only indicate the path. The guru says the 'eye of the eye' sees; he does not provide special powers but guides the student to use his mind and intellect to grasp what this eye of the eye could be. Since Truth has no qualities and intellect can understand only qualities, it is necessary that one develops intuition, the instrument for identifying the Atman, Truth. The vehicle of light is not intellect, but intuition.

Atman is distinct from the known, that is, the phenomenal world; and is above the unknown or other than the unknown, as the Atman is the knower, seer and witness. Due to the Atman, speech is uttered and stops at death when the Atman leaves the body. Speech cannot illuminate Truth, though it is illumined by it. The absolute all-pervading pure existence Truth is Brahman, "not this that you worship" says the Upanishad. From this we are to understand that the Gods and Deities are not Brahman. One needs to go beyond name and form to find the essence or tattva. Thus, in order to express the ultimate divinity Brahman, the guru provides suggestions in indicative vocabulary.

The mind cannot of its own even feel spirituality, but only due to its nearness to the Atman within. Thought flow too functions only in the presence of the Atman. Atman directs the ear towards its object, sound and thereby thoughts follow. Words cannot express the roaring silence of Pure Consciousness and nor can we perceive it with our mind and intellect. What we can perceive is a relative reality, the conditioned Atman. The sadhak must realise the real Atman through sadhana "for himself, by himself, in himself". For the time that Atman is not pervading any name and form, the form is dead matter and not a living entity.

The guru warns the student not to be overconfident with what he has learnt so far. The disciple is unable to express in words his inner intuitive experience of Reality. The difficulty felt by him at the moment of pure God consciousness, is that there is no I-ness and the moment he is aware of his I-ness, he is no longer experiencing God consciousness. Where the ego is felt, God is not there. The guru goes on to explain what Atman is. Pure Atman cannot be known, as it is the Knowing Principle. In the reflected light of the Atman, the ego is created and when the ego is ended, only Atman remains. There is no 'I' at the end of a successful Sadhana. One can meditate oneself into the Truth and merge in it. This merger is possible, is the daring assertion of all the seers, as per Vedanta.

The subjective experience of self-awareness, of Pure Consciousness, is the experience of the pure Atman. A true Vedantin is a balanced individual, with an equally powerful mind and intellect and a third developed divine power called intuition, through which the Atman is experienced. Intuitively the mind recognises the Atman as the witness of the three states of consciousness waking, dream and deep sleep and as a continuity of awareness Atman pervades all three.

It is necessary here that we reiterate what we have learnt so far, before we go on to a very interesting short story described in the Kenopanishad. Atman illumines thought, but is distinct from thought, as all changes are in the thought flow, not in the Atman, Truth. All painful experiences in life are due to the ego and the phenomenal world, both of which are unreal. Realising Brahman while living in this world as a human being, is the achievement of all human aspirations and one's final goal. Not achieving this means that one's life as a human being is wasted. So, by striving, the sage sees the same Atman in all beings and giving up the life of the senses, becomes immortal. Once the Self, Atman is realised, one knows God and becomes God even in this very life, here and now. Death is no longer fearsome and one accepts it like a change of clothes, as expressed beautifully in the Bhagwad Gita.

In a final effort to caution the disciple from assuming pride in learning the theoretical knowledge of Brahman, a short story is here entered into regarding the five Deities or Gods of the five sense organs, who are the five great elements and their relationship with Brahman.

Once upon a time, so the story goes, Brahman fought a battle and overpowered the demons on behalf of the Gods. The Gods, however, became proud asserting that they had been victorious. Brahman learnt of this and came before them in the form of a Yaksha. The gods asked Agni, the God of fire to approach him and find out who he is. Agni spoke of his power to burn before Brahman but was unable to even burn a blade of grass and returned. Next Vayu, the wind God was similarly vanquished as he could not blow and move a blade of grass. Finally, Indra, the chief of Gods went to the place where the Yaksha was, only to find that he had vanished. Indra waited patiently and was rewarded by the appearance of the Goddess Uma, the daughter of the snowy mountain Himavan. Uma explained that the Yaksha was the great spirit, Brahman, himself and he had ensured the victory over the demons in the battle.

A vivid description is given here of Brahman's manifestation of his cosmic powers as a comparison with that of the Gods as: "shone forth like the splendour of lightening" and "he disappeared within the twinkling of an eye". Also described is Brahman as Atman within the body: "as one thinks of Brahman by the mind and as speedily as the mind wills".

Let us understand why Indra was successful, whereas Agni and Vayu were not. Indra went in meek surrender, without arrogance and pride and with an earnest desire to learn the truth and thus waited patiently. He was briefed by Uma about the Truth- Brahman. Both Agni and Vayu boasted of their powers and lost out due to their pride.

Often disciples in their vanity and impatience, witness the disappearance of their goal, Brahman when they are very near to it. They require inner calm and fully awakened awareness, together with divine determination and an alert and vigilant intellect. It is only through patience and perseverance that one can achieve the aim of seeking truth. The process of detaching oneself from the unreal, the false ego and taking up concentration and inner purification is the way to self-perfection; also gaining personal conviction that one is the Atman.

The sadhak needs to reach the Indra 'Stithi', a condition where he is in "a passionate eagerness to understand, humbleness and selflessness in his seeking and inexhaustible faith" in his success. It is explained by the Upanishad that the first few subjective experiences of truth come in "flashes" quick and sudden that only an alert disciple will catch. Therefore, the terms lightening and twinkling are used.

When the mind is silent, Brahman reveals itself. There is a silence between thoughts that arise in the mind and when the mind is concentrating on the Atman, thoughts slow down and in one of the silences between thoughts, Atman flashes its existence into the sadhak's awareness.

The guru offers Tadvanam as an option to be meditated upon by the disciple, as the all- pervading spirit. Worship and

Upasana are means of purifying and perfecting the student's inner instruments, the mind and intellect and once this is accomplished, one needs deeper and more intense meditation. Meditating thus one becomes what one meditates upon-Tadvanam, the all- pervading spirit.

On a query raised by the disciple regarding the technique of self- perfection, he is thus answered; realisation being the watchword of Vedanta, the Upanishad provides information to the last detail, for the disciple to progress on his path. Truth rests on austerity, self-restraint and dedicated selfless work. Living with what one needs, rather than what one wants, leads to the ideal of austerity. Self-control in all matters, pursuing the good rather than the pleasurable, ensures self-restraint. Dedicated selfless work is following one's dharma and karma, which includes prayer, jaap repeating God's name and dhyan meditation. Finally, "Truth is Truth's abode" and thus a sadhak must value every bit of education, knowledge and experience, as they help him on his pilgrimage to the inner sanctum of Truth.

Kenopanishad ends with the assertion that the one who knows the Reality, destroys ignorance and is established in Truth, Brahman the Highest and the Blissful. He has gained Self- Knowledge, the fundamental basis of Vedanta.

BHAGWAD GITA UPANISHAD

A few words to express the glory of this Upanishad are penned below by the author.

Bhagwad Gita you are gracious,

Your knowledge is spacious.

Immanent in every speck,

Reality as Brahman does reflect.

Touching truth in all its facets,

Places purity above all assets.

Sadhana, dhyan and meditation,

Lead the way to Self-realisation.

Om Tat Sat most sacred mantra,

Om is the Reality,

Tat is That spirituality,

Sat is good and auspiciousness.

The Reality is near and far,

It is moving and unmoving,

It is not Sat and not Asat,

Reality is Om Tat Sat.

The fire is Brahman,

Oblations are Brahman,

One conducting puja is Brahman,

The One invoked is Brahman.

One whose thoughts are absorbed in Brahman,

Such a one alone attains Brahman.

Ashwattha tree is inverted,

As its roots rest in Brahman.

Its green leaves are human beings,

Born, existing, dying as dry leaves.

Branches ongoing human actions and desires,

Unattachment that quenches all the fires.

Three spiritual paths of Bhakti, Karma and Gyan,

They each reach the pinnacle of dhyan.

With knowledge of Para and Apara Prakriti,

The seeker worships Para and drops Apara Prakriti.

Apara or matter including ego need spirit to come alive,

Para or spirit is independent and alone does survive.

Kshetrajna, Purush, Brahman, Atman,

Self, Aum and Pure Consciousness

Are various names of the Ultimate Reality.

They illumine all that we know,

Realise intuitively and experience spiritually.

Krishna manifested in human form,

To awaken man to Vedanta's call.

Ved Vyasa, one of the greatest rishis of Bharatvarsh, related the dialogue between Arjun, one of the Pandu princes of Hastinapur with his friend, philosopher and guide Krishna. At the beginning of this conversation, Arjun was not aware of the true identity of Krishna as God himself, who had taken up human form for the sake of mankind. As an integral part of the Mahabharat, the Bhagwad Gita contains the essence of the prominent Upanishads and illuminates the mind of the reader on all the essentials of the spiritual findings of the Vedic Rishis. Written more than four thousand years ago, it is as relevant today as it was then, since it takes up all the human doubts one by one and clarifies them in depth. Arjun's dilemma is our dilemma.

The setting is in the middle of a battlefield in Kurukshetra, where Arjun's hundred cousins are the opponents, having taken over territory unlawfully belonging to Arjun and his four brothers. It must be borne in mind that just as the battlefield showcases a war between the righteous Pandu princes with the unrighteous Kaurav cousins, so also one's mind is regularly the battlefield, where disputes between right and wrong are settled.

On seeing his uncles, teachers, brothers- in- law, cousin brothers and other relatives and friends ready to fight against him, Arjun is suddenly overtaken by grief at the thought of killing them. Arjun sits down in his chariot, putting down his bow and arrows and exclaims to Krishna, his charioteer that he will not fight. The dialogue that ensues with Krishna admonishing Arjun for his faint- hearted weakness that he is projecting as a virtue, the Bhagwad Gita Upanishad begins.

Realising that he is confused and unable to take a correct decision, Arjun requests Krishna to guide him. Krishna begins to explain the ancient philosophy of Sankhya Yoga or the Knowledge of the Self or Atman within each human being. The Self is eternal and does not die. Since only the body dies, there is no reason to grieve. The Self leaves one body and takes on another body, just as one takes off old clothes and wears new ones. Also, when the body is slain, the Self is not slain. The Self cannot be cut, burnt, wet or dried. The Self is eternal and all pervading, stable and firm, indestructible and unborn. In case one believes that the Self is born and dies, there is no reason to grieve because anything that is born must die. If birth is certain, so is death and if death is certain, so is rebirth.

Arjun is a member of the Kshatriya caste and it is his duty or Dharma to fight for the territory and subjects which are rightfully theirs; the Kauravs their opponents are unjust rulers while the Pandavs are just rulers and must protect their subjects. Also, in view of the details of Sankhya Yoga already described by Krishna, Arjun is told to take up his duty as a warrior without looking towards the results of his actions. In this way he will break the bondage that action brings and he will be free from the results of karma. Controlling his senses (Dama) and his mind (Sama), he must work with a calm, steady and stable attitude. Such evenness of mind is called Samatvam. This yoga is efficiency in action, using productive efficiency without and spiritual efficiency within.

On Arjun's request to know how a Realised person behaves, Krishna also explains how he achieves this state. A realised master is blissful, desireless and established in steady wisdom. He is content in the Atman and pure consciousness. He is free from anger, attachment and fear. He is like the ocean, undisturbed even when rivers of desires flow into him. He attains absolute freedom and is no longer tormented by the dualities of honour and dishonour, cold and heat. He does not run after pleasure or wealth and uses his vivek (discrimination) to segregate the Shreya (good) from preya (pleasant). He is content within himself, contemplating on the Atman and as such it is day for him. The worldly person, attached to material goods, relatives and friends is not interested in the internal world or Atman. Thus, what is day to the Yogi is night to the worldly person and vice versa. The yogi can no longer be deluded, as he is now one with Brahman.

With a view to encourage Arjun to walk on the spiritual path, Krishna speaks to Arjun of three paths to choose from, Karma yoga, Bhakti yoga and Gyan yoga according to one's temperament. All three paths are attempts to purify the mind and make it calm, steady and single pointed. No matter which path is taken up, the final experience of Pure Consciousness at the moment of enlightenment, is the same. Let us take them up one by one.

Karma yoga is work in a spirit of self-sacrifice, dedication and service. Arjun wanted to give up his duty, due to his attachment to relatives, instead of controlling his emotions and acting with vivek and true renunciation, selflessly. Krishna tells Arjun that he is not ready for the path of Gyan yoga and meditation and should take up action without attachment, in order to become a Karma yogi. He goes on to say that man is deluded by anger and desire, which reside in the senses, mind and intellect. The body is gross and the senses are superior to the body as they are subtle, mind is superior to the senses and intellect to the mind and finally the Atman to the intellect. Thus, knowing the Atman is the subtlest and most superior, one should get rid of the desires from the senses, mind and intellect and concentrate on the Atman alone.

The next step after Karma yoga is Karma Sanyasa, which is renunciation of action. One can give up something only if one has it. So only after achieving karma yoga with a mind and intellect purified and developed for steady contemplation and also fit for higher meditation, can one take up Karma Sanyasa. Karma Sanyasa means giving up ego and desire prompted actions. Such a mental attitude, ensures the divine within, observes the outward actions; while the ego acting through the gunas of Prakriti (nature) takes the merits and demerits of the actions performed. The ego goes through the cycle of rebirth, whereas the Atman, the observer, does not. Krishna tells us that one can then take up the path of knowledge or Gyan yoga. Meditating on Atman or Brahman, will lead one to Brahman and once having reached the Ultimate Reality one does not revert to ignorance.

Krishna points out that one should not care for the result of an action undertaken, as then the result will neither affect nor bind one. Actions are of three kinds viz. Right actions, forbidden actions and lastly inaction. Actions are caused by desires and it is important to understand the motive or emotion behind them. In case the motive is selfishness, then it is a forbidden action. An action done with no interest in the result, with neither an emotional, mental or intellectual clinging to the expected fruits or results, it is a right action. In deep sleep one does not act at all and neither does one improve nor deteriorate, as the mind and intellect are absent and therefore this is inaction.

Life can become filled with right actions if offered without attachment to results, with love and shraddha to Brahman as a sacrifice or puja. In the puja the fire, the offering, the persons conducting the puja and the one invoked are all Brahman. A person whose thoughts are absorbed in Brahman alone, attains Brahman.

Other methods such as pranayama, controlling the breath; leading a life of self-control through restraining the senses; concentration of the mind in Atman and gifts, penance and decrease of food intake can help in steadying the mind through constant practice. The best of all is the Fire of Knowledge, which burns away all actions and one attains freedom, as actions no longer bind. In case one does not take up any of the paths, one continues to live in the cycle of births and deaths, so Krishna declares.

Concentration or dhyan requires that one sits in a clean place, not too high or low with a cotton cloth placed over a warm cloth. Sitting erect and firmly one should fix the gaze on the tip of the nose and concentrate the mind on the Atman or Self. Moderation in movement and action, eating and sleeping is recommended for a seeker. Withdrawing one's senses and concentrating on the Supreme, one should think of nothing else. In case the mind wanders, it must be brought back with calmness, diligence and patience till such time the mind becomes tranquil. Slowly the mind gets identified with Brahman and one experiences infinite bliss. Krishna confirms that though it seems impossible, it can be achieved through practice and dispassion.

Arjun wants to know what happens if a person on the spiritual path dies before he attains Self-realisation. Krishna assures him that such a person is not lost, but is reborn in a suitable environment and or family, where he continues on the spiritual path. Ultimately, even after some rebirths, he reaches Brahman.

One who lives constantly in the awareness that it is the Atman within that illuminates the body, mind, intellect and their functions, is one who knows his own true nature. On death, the body disintegrates into the five elements but the subtle thoughts, impressions remain in an un- manifest form as vasanas and due to this, rebirth in a suitable environment takes place. It is only when one rediscovers the Atman within through sincere sadhana, that one is not born again. Choosing the path of light and Shreya (good) and using dispassion, unattachment, discriminative thinking, selfless karma and worship, the meditator rises to higher and higher levels, till at last the Atman is realised.

Krishna tells Arjun that His nature or Prakriti is twofold. The higher is Para Prakriti pure spirit and the lower is Apara Prakriti made up of the five elements of space, air, fire, water and earth plus mind, intellect and ego. Matter or lower Prakriti depends on spirit for its existence and functioning, but spirit does not depend on matter for anything, as Pure Spirit, Atman, Brahman IS. Prakriti also has the power of veiling called Maya, which uses its qualities of Sattva, Rajas and Tamas to enable the entities of the world interact amongst themselves and simultaneously hides the Para Prakriti from them. One needs to go even beyond Sattva to reach the Atman, unless one is content to live with the outside world that seems so real due to the veil of delusion cast by Maya.

Four kinds of persons worship God: the distressed, seekers of knowledge, seekers of wealth and spiritually wise, the gyani. The first three receive what they desire through the Deva worshipped by them. However, these are temporary and only the gyani finally gains Brahman. To such a man of perfection everything becomes clear, he comes to know Krishna, who in reality is Brahman. He is the elements and sacrifices as well. Knowledge without wisdom is of little use. Every aspect of life is mixed up and one has to separate truth from untruth, reality from falsity by using vivek (discrimination)!

In order to take up the Bhakti marg, one just needs to love the divine within and allow it to manifest itself as Pure Consciousness. When one takes the first steps on this path a fixed time for prayers, going to the temple or satsang is a must. Slowly one finds that the mind is constantly on the Almighty and when one sits for meditation or chanting, the mind has become peaceful and attentive and is always connected to God. The gyani feels he is Brahman, whereas the bhakt sees God as separate from him, as an entity he worships. In a comparison between the paths of Gyan, where one sees the unmanifest Brahman and that of Bhakti, where one reaches out to the personal God in the personification of Krishna, the Bhakti marg is considered easier as one can comfortably worship a tangible God in the familiar human form vis – a – vis an unmanifest God. In fact, the Bhakti marg is recommended for the people who are attached to their identity with their body, me and mine. The devotee is told to put his mind on the idol of his Ishta Devta or Krishna and next using his intellect see the Pure Spirit behind the idol. Thus, His presence can be felt through constant and devoted progress on this path. A sincere devotee has the following qualities says Krishna: he is silent, content, forgiving, not agitated, free from egoism and attachment, does not hate, grieve or desire.

Krishna now begins to express what Brahman really is. He states that He is the unattached ever free Brahman, the substratum of all beings, but does not identify with them nor dwell in them. Even human beings do not dwell or exist in Him but only rest in Him, as air rests in space. God is the inactive Brahman and is the witness, while His nature, the active Prakriti does all the actions of projecting, maintaining and dissolving the universe and beings. Arjun is asked to fill his thoughts with Brahman, in order to ensure the evolution of the mind for spiritual growth and thus endeavour to divinise his thoughts, a crucial requirement in all three Bhakti, Karma and Gyan margs.

Through the power of manifestation called 'Vibhuti' one can see and experience the beings and things around one. God is immutable and does not change in this process. He is the origin of all and the world evolves from Him. Some of the qualities in human beings that arise from Him are truth, calmness, fear, fame etc. God is the seed and essence of all. One may like to take up some more examples so that further clarity will ensue: the sun, jaap, yagna, syllable Aum, Narada Devrishi, time, death, the power of the powerful, silence of secrets, Vyasa Muni, ocean, mind Himalayas etc. In fact, the essence in ego and the creator/ projector Brahma is the same.

Just as in electricity there is no heat or light but when it passes through an electric heater or bulb it provides both. In this way, Krishna has taught the art of seeing the unseen in the seen. See Brahman, Pure Consciousness, Krishna, the Divine by meditating on any of His manifestations that surround one.

Arjun asks to see Krishna's Virat or Vishwa rupa and Krishna accedes to his request providing him with divine eyesight. The vision is immense and all pervading, brilliant as if a thousand suns have risen together. It is terrifying too, as it depicts a thousand hands, many mouths, legs and feet. Many persons are rushing into a mouth full of fire, while some Devas are frightened and are saying 'peace' countless times. The vision is awe inspiring and fearful. It portrays a continuous movement showing birth, old age and death. Arjun filled with fear at this stupendous sight, requests Krishna to once again assume His normal form. Krishna obliges and then explains to Arjun that the destroyer and (kaal) Time is God Himself and not Arjun and therefore he should get up and do his duty of fighting the war. He is only an instrument and not the doer or karta.

Brahman, Pure Consciousness, Self or Atman which is Spirit in human beings is also called Kshetrajna and Purush and is the knower of Kshetra, the field which is made up of matter, and all its activities. The Self illuminates all that we know intellectually, realise intuitively and experience spiritually. It also illumines both light and the experience of darkness. The body or kshetra is inert and only the Life Principle, the Atman or Self makes it conscious and functioning. Kshetrajna or Self is also the perceiving principle in all the sense equipments of ear, eye, tongue, skin and nose, as also the mind and intellect. It has "hands and feet" everywhere. Self, conditioned by the mind is ego, unconditioned is Brahman!

Upanishads excel in double meaning phrases that depict Brahman in opposite positions or conditions, in order to entice the seeker to apply oneself to unravelling the mystery of the Almighty, that cannot be easily described. Bhagwad Gita is no exception. Self is both "moving and unmoving" because It does not move, only the vehicle it resides in moves.

Self is "near and far" as it exists in every form around us and far as it exists in reality in Supreme Truth far away from us, since one can know It only through Self Realisation.

Self is not Sat (Being) nor is It Asat (non- Being). It is not Sat because one cannot perceive it and not Asat, as it can be perceived in the world which it manifests.

Purush when identified with matter is ego and goes on a whirlwind trip of birth, death, birth and so on, suffering sorrow and pain, till it throws off the ego to be the divine Self as Purush once again. One who realises within himself the difference between what is matter and spirit, does not collect any new vasanas (impressions) and the old ones die the moment one gets Self Realisation. If one continues in this state, on one's death one is not born again.

The spirit is One and is the same in every individual but Prakriti or nature is different in each due to the vasanas (past impressions and experiences). This is due to the three gunas or moods or attitudes of Sattva, Rajas and Tamas inherent in Prakriti. Each person must endeavour to rise from Tamas-'moh' or extreme identity and attachment to one's body to Rajas –activity to Sattva-luminosity. One needs to transcend even Sattva and become Gunatitta. Also, one should learn to stand apart and witness the activities of the gunas as they interact with those of others, without identifying with their moods.

The concept of the Ashwattha tree, taken from the Kathopanishad, declares that Brahman being the source of the world is its roots and thus the tree is inverted. Knowledge contained in the Vedas is the branches extending below. Branches extending outward are human actions, buds are fresh desires, leaves are human beings- born, existing, dying. The tree lives on eternally while all beings come and go. One can look at this tree as a continuous hell from which one wants deliverance and one can cut it with the sword of non-attachment. The other point of view is that this world comes from Brahman and is wholly Brahman itself and one must love and accept it as God manifest, seeing God everywhere in people, animals, things and the fire elements.

One knows that the gross body is perishable and is destroyed but the immortal Atman lives on, to move to another body taking the senses and the mind with it, just as the wind carries the scent from the flowers. It is the senses that experience joy or sorrow, not the body. In order to understand how the subtle body moves from one gross body to another, one needs to acquire the "eye of wisdom" through Sadhana and meditation.

The art of living is an exercise in discrimination at every step so that such traits are developed in one's individual character that will lead to a life of purity and serenity. When one assesses one's nature, it will be found to contain some demoniac traits as well. The spiritually inclined person will strive to imbibe noble qualities, while the materialistic minded person caught up in the three gates of hell - lust, greed and anger, goes on a pleasure hunt. Krishna points to the urgency of character building to enable one to move on the spiritual path. There are others who feel that they live a good life by having faith and taking up good thoughts and actions and see no need to study the scriptures. After explaining the three kinds of faith, shraddha and tapas, austerities. Daan (charity) and sacrifice (yagna), Krishna aware that human beings are not infallible, provided them with a mantra 'Om Tat Sat' and explained its message and usage. Om or Aum is the reality, Brahman. Aum is present in waking, dream and deep sleep states and is also the Pranav used before each mantra ensuring the purity of the sacrifice or charity performed. Tat is 'That Reality' or great truth not visible to one's senses. Sat is good, reality or auspicious act. All austerities, sacrifices or charity should be undertaken with faith, as one done without it would be Asat or meaningless.

Tyaga and Sanyasa are terms often used by Krishna to Arjun and He explains their meaning as follows. Tyaga is the giving up of sensory filled lower impulses in one's moment to moment contact with life. Sanyasa is the final giving up of the finite, in the total awareness of the Infinite as the Truth of life. Continuous practice of Tyaga prepares one for Sanyasa. Through Tyaga done with the correct mental attitude by giving up attachment and the fruits, one improves the 'buddhi shakti' or intellect power and the 'medha shakti' or psychic intelligence which brings about vivek (discrimination) in one's actions.

In order to ensure that one is comfortable doing the work that is assigned to one and can reach perfection in it, the four castes of Brahmin, Kshatriya, Vaishya and Shudra were introduced, based on the disposition or gunas expressed in individual personalities. These castes were not hereditary. Offering one's actions to God and fixing one's mind on God, knowing that the same Atman resides in everyone, through God's grace one experiences Brahman!

Krishna clarified all Arjun's doubts and provided him with the secret knowledge of the infinite Reality, Brahman and in the light of the aforesaid, now asks him to take his own decision regarding how he wishes to act. Arjun now knows the reality behind his friend Krishna and fortified with the true knowledge of his Self, tells Krishna that he will fight the battle. One must understand that one is privileged to hear the conversation, the doubts and the clarifications between Krishna and Arjun as one has gained infinite knowledge that one can share with like- minded persons. Remember the answers to one's questions and prayers always come from within, from one's charioteer.

EPILOGUE

Silence does in silence dwell,

Truth got hidden as night fell.

Along the shady lane did walk,

A seeker alone and did not talk.

Truth peeped out from the mountainside

Astonished at the silence, he could not hide.

The seeker was seated lost in prayer,

The birds their twitter did not dare.

The forest and all the animals abide,

In silence wondering if the seeker is alive.

Truth is impatient to meet the person,

Takes a few steps towards his position.

Steeped in the depth of Aatmic silence,

Sadhak meets Truth without his I-ness.

As Truth and Sadhak are face to face,

Sadhak merges in Truth, blessed by his grace.

Silence does in silence dwell,

Truth, Bliss, Pure Consciouness forever revel.

The silence between two consecutive Aums chanted by a seeker is called Turiya, the fourth plane of consciousness of Aum. Turiya is the substratum of the three stages of 'A' waking, 'U' dream and 'M' deep sleep and it also transcends the three to become the Absolute Divine, the Aum equivalent to Brahman. Brahman is Atman and Atman is Self. Brahman is Satchitananda, the Truth, Pure Consciousness and Bliss. Nirguna, without name and form, pure divinity, the gyani tells us is our ultimate goal to be realised in this life. I offer my heartfelt good wishes and prayer for all those desirous of a glimpse of Satchitananda, here and now.

9 789354 462054